15 BATTLES THAT CHANGED THE WORLD

The history of mankind is too frequently the history of man's wars, for armed conflict has shaped the history of the world. On this note, Robert Silverberg tells the stories of 15 of the world's decisive battles; battles which have been turning points in wars as well as in history. Beginning with the Battle of Marathon and continuing chronologically to the Battle of Stalingrad, the author describes each battle graphically. The battles Mr. Silverberg has chosen to illustrate the course of history are those he feels have been vitally important to the history of the world and at the same time have accomplished something. A major portion of the text is devoted to clarifying the political results, plus some speculation on what might have happened had the tide of each battle been reversed.

15 BATTLES

THAT CHANGED THE WORLD

by Robert Silverberg

illustrated by Lewis Zacks

G. P. Putnam's Sons

New York

To Robert A. W. Lowndes

CONTENTS

INTRODUCTION

EVERYONE agrees that war is a brutal and unpleasant business. Why, then, write books about it? Why read them? Why not ignore the whole ugly concept and hope that it will go away?

History would be a much more cheerful subject if there had been no wars. It is pleasant to think of a world without violence, a world where the lion lies down with the lamb, and swords are beaten into plowshares. Perhaps—although it looks less likely all the time—humanity will someday attain such a happy state. A backward look, though, tells us that for the last six thousand years, since the beginning of recorded history, the natural occupation of mankind appears to have been waging war. Over the broad perspective of history, the interludes of peace seem very few and far between.

A history of mankind, then, quickly becomes a history of man's wars. Armed conflict again and again has been the touchstone by which the trends of history were developed. Sad, perhaps, but true—and only a fool closes his eyes to the truth, unpleasant to behold though it may be.

So in this book we study man as a creature of bloodshed. It's a melancholy prospect, but there is one redeeming factor. Hard as it may be to believe, things have been getting better all the time. The world has come through a purifying bath of blood to emerge more civilized than ever before.

This may seem like a startling statement in a world where words like "overkill," "megaton," and "fallout" fill the headlines of the newspapers. But I think it stands up. True, we are better able to destroy one another than ever before. True, a war of unparalleled savagery and butchery was fought less than twenty years ago. True, friction and anger flare up constantly between nations.

But despite all these depressing throwbacks to a more vicious era, I think we have progressed. We have reached certain moral beliefs about the nature of war that simply did not exist in centuries past. Look at the history of the ancient kingdom of Assyria, for example: for hundreds of years, this nation made war on its neighbors for the simple joy of killing and looting. The law of the sword was the only law in that ancient time. City fought city; man's only loyalty was to his family, and sometimes to his local overlord.

We have higher loyalties today. Loyalty to the city has given way to loyalty to the nation and, let us hope, to loyalty to mankind, loyalty to the world. We are not a perfect people yet, not by any means. It is quite conceivable that the world will have been blown to smithereens before anyone can read the page I have just written, and that is a sad commentary on the state of our alleged civilization. But I am hopeful. I think we have been moving in the right direction over the past six thousand years. Sometimes we have taken one step backward for every two steps forward, and at other times we have taken two steps backward for every forward one. Progress has been slow and uneven. But there has been progress.

This book is the record of that progress. If it has any unifying theme, it is the story of the victory of light over darkness, of the triumph of the forces of liberty over those of tyranny. There are exceptions. The Battle of Adrianople, for instance, was a victory for the side of chaos. But most of the battles you will read about in the pages to come are landmarks in the struggle of freedom against despotism. Inch by inch, mankind crawled forward out of superstition and slavery. The task was a great one, and could not be accomplished by peaceful means. Those who wish peace must sometimes shed blood to achieve it, and this is the great paradox of civilization.

Why 15 battles?

I must confess that this is a purely arbitrary number. One could choose 20 decisive battles of history just as sensibly, or 25, or 50. Fifteen has the virtue of being compact: the highlights of history can be understandably investigated, without dragging in an infinite number of secondary conflicts.

There is also a certain sentimental reason for choosing 15 great battles. The first of all books of this type chose that number: Sir Edward S. Creasy's *The Fifteen Decisive Battles of the World*, first published in 1851 and one of the masterpieces of historical writing. Opinions differ on historical matters, and only eight of Creasy's battles have found their way into this book. (Two of my 15 were fought after Creasy wrote.) More than a century after Creasy, it seemed appropriate to me to choose the same number of battles, each a major turning point in the evolution of today's world.

Not every book of this kind sticks to Creasy's classic number of 15, though. One in particular is far more all-embracing, and I recommend it here to anyone who wishes to read the complete story of mankind's military conflicts. This is *A Military History of the Western World,* by Major General J. F. C. Fuller. In three huge volumes, General Fuller brilliantly sketches the entire story of war from earliest times to 1944. There is no better book on the subject.

Two more preliminary points need to be mentioned. The first is that the present book does not pretend to be an account of the entire world's 15 most decisive battles, but simply the decisive battles of the *western* world—that is, the world of Europe and North America. Fierce struggles have taken place in other parts of the world, between Turk and Arab, between Mongol and Chinese, between tribesmen in Africa, between islanders in Polynesia. Some of these battles have had permanent impact on the histories of those areas. But they have had no direct bearing on the development of our part of the world, and so they have been omitted here. Too many historians forget to point out that they are dealing only with one special segment of their subject. There is more to the history of music than Bach, Beethoven and Brahms, more to the story of art than Rembrandt and Titian and Picasso. And there is far more to the world's military history than these 15 battles.

The second point is that I have tried to choose only decisive battles—turning points not only in a war but in history itself. That is why some seemingly minor battles, involving only a few thousand men on each side, have been included, while World War I has been completely ignored. Sometimes a clash of a couple of battalions has remade the flow of history. World War I, for all its millions of victims, decided nothing. The historians of five hundred years hence, if there are any, will probably view that war as simply the chaotic prelude to World War II. In itself it was nothing but a costly, disastrous stalemate. Nor were any of its individual battles decisive in the proper way. It was a war that simply ground to a clanking halt when all parties were too weary to go on—and continued again, in a far more bloody way, a quarter of a century later.

No one's list of the 15 decisive battles of western history will be quite like anyone else's. In the chapters that follow, I present mine. The list is open to attack and debate, and I hope it will receive attack and debate. Unquestioning acceptance of the opinions of others, I think, is one of the most serious sins an intelligent being can commit.

THE BATTLE OF MARATHON

*The Greeks
Learn Their Own Strength*

THE early history of man is a record of tyranny. The Egyptians, the Assyrians, the Babylonians were warlike peoples whose empires were founded on the dream of conquest. The Assyrians in particular specialized in destruction, pillage and murder on a grand scale.

The dream of these ancient empires was one that is still with some nations today: the dream of world dominion. "The world," from the Assyrian point of view, meant a relatively small area of the Near East, but they were determined to make themselves masters of all they surveyed, and for a time they succeeded.

The Assyrians met with bloody retribution, eventually. Their cities were sacked and their empire destroyed. But the idea of world dominion did not die with them. Just as they had emerged to triumph over earlier races, so did a new race come to sit in the throne of Assyria.

This new race of despots came down out of the mountains of Iran. Tribal warfare had forged a single nation out of Medians, Lydians and Persians, and by the seventh century before Christ, the Persian Empire was a power to be reckoned with in the oriental world. Assyria soon fell to the newcomers, and then Babylonia. By the time of Cyrus the Great, who ruled from 559 B.C. to 530, Persia was the supreme power of the world.

Like many nations which rise rapidly to supremacy, the Persian Empire had no time to develop an art or culture of its own. Persians borrowed their art from Assyrians, who in turn had stolen most of their ideas from the older kingdom of Babylonia. The Persians borrowed the bloodthirstiness of Assyria, too. Despotism was the order of the day. The ruined palaces of Persia provide us with portraits of the kings—hawk-nosed, fiery-eyed men with curling beards, stiff and solemn and fearsome. Cyrus and Darius and Xerxes of Persia look very much like the Assyrian tyrants, Sennacherib and Ashurbanipal and Sargon, whose portraits we also have.

Cambyses II, the son of Cyrus, attempted to extend Persian sway to that part of the world Cyrus had not managed to conquer. Cambyses marched on Egypt and made the Pharaoh his slave. He conquered Ethiopia and other regions of Africa. But then revolts in his own country cut short his career of world conquest. He was forced to return to Persia to quell a series of uprisings.

Cambyses died without an heir. In the confusion that followed, Darius, a member of the royal family, was able to seize the throne. Triumphantly he marched the length and breadth of the Persian Empire, restoring order. And then he extended Persian dominion to new lands on all sides. It seemed as though all the world would fall beneath the heel of the conquerors.

One nation resisted.

It is not really accurate to speak of the Greeks of 500 B.C. as a nation, not in our sense of the word. Rather, Greece was a collection of cities where a common language was spoken. There was no central government. Each city went its own way, frequently warring against its neighbor.

The Greek cities were ruled by kings—tyrants, they were called, though the word does not have today's meaning of cruelty and oppression. Some of the Greek tyrants were truly tyrannical; others were wise and just rulers.

There was an idea in Greece, an idea that was new to the world. It was the idea of democracy—rule by the *demos*, the people. It was a new idea, a dangerous idea, a subversive idea. Elsewhere in the world, the people meekly submitted to the whims of their kings. In the Greek cities, though, a harsh and dictatorial ruler might be cast out by the people. Some of the cities even had legislative assemblies, elected by the people, to help the king make the laws. This was all very strange elsewhere in the world. In Persia, as in Assyria and Egypt, the ruler had held the power of life and death over his subjects. In some of the cities of Greece, the ruler served his people, rather than commanded them.

Darius I found the Greeks uncomfortable neighbors. At that time the Greeks dwelled not only on their own peninsula but in Asia Minor, or Ionia. Darius had absorbed the Ionian cities into his empire easily enough. But, unexpectedly, the Ionians rebelled against Persian domination, and the Greek cities on the other side of the Aegean Sea sent aid to their cousins of Ionia.

Twenty-five Greek ships, 20 of them from Athens, crossed the sea and sent warriors inland, in 498 B.C. In a surprising gesture the Greeks captured the Persian city of Sardis and burned it. The Persians soon drove the invaders out, but it was an insult such as the Persians had never before suffered. The Greek historian Herodotus, in his account of the struggle between the Greeks and Persians, wrote:

"Now when it was told to King Darius that Sardis had been taken and burnt by the Athenians and Ionians, he took small heed of the Ionians, well knowing who they were, and that their revolt would soon be put down; but he asked who, and what manner of men, the Athenians were. And when he had been told, he called for his bow; and, having taken it, and placed an arrow on the string, he let the arrow fly towards heaven; and as he shot it into the air, he said, 'O Supreme God! Grant me that I may avenge myself on the Athenians.' And when he had said this, he appointed one of his servants to say to him every day as he sat at meat, 'Sire, remember the Athenians.' "

The Athenians were a very special manner of men indeed. In 510 B.C. they had driven out the tyrant Hippias and had set up a democracy. Hippias fled to the court of Darius, and Athens enjoyed the benefits of justice and law. By today's standards we would not call Athens a very democratic state, since slavery flourished, women had no legal rights, and only the wealthy men of the city were allowed to vote. But the democratic idea was new and unique, and Athens was far more advanced than any other state of its era.

Darius longed to smash these troublesome Athenians. Hippias, at his court, urged the great king to conquer Athens and reinstate him as its ruler. First, however, Darius had to quell the Ionian rebellion. It was not until 492 B.C., six years after the burning of Sardis, that Darius was free to deal with the Athenians.

In that year he dispatched a fleet to Greece, 600 ships strong. A severe storm, though, sent half the ships to destruction, and cost the Persians 20,000 men. It was an evil omen for Darius' conquest of Greece but, determined, he ordered his forces to be rebuilt for a second attempt.

While the Persians assembled their forces, Darius sent heralds to the cities of Greece. "Surrender now," he told them. "Avoid destruction by swearing allegiance to Persia."

Many of the smaller Greek cities, frightened by Darius' might, bowed to the order. Athens, though, haughtily refused, as did Sparta, the other great Greek city, and Eretria, which had joined with Athens in the raid on Sardis in 498.

The maddened Darius ordered his armies to crush the obstinate Greek cities. The Persian army landed on Greek soil in 490 B.C., under the joint command of Datis, a Median general, and Artaphernes, nephew of Darius. They were commanded to destroy Athens and Eretria, and lead their people into Persia as slaves.

The Persian army moved through Greece without meeting resistance, and laid siege to Eretria. The city resisted bravely for six days, but on the seventh pro-Persian traitors within the walls treacherously admitted the invading army. The temples of Eretria were burned in revenge for the burning of Sardis, and the population was shipped to Persia to be enslaved.

While Artaphernes, with part of the Persian force, was besieging Eretria, Datis was leading an attack on Athens. The Athenians immediately sent a messenger to Sparta, 150 miles to the south, asking for help. The messenger, whose name was Pheidippides, covered the distance in just two days. He reached Sparta on September 9, 490 B.C.

The Spartans, as allies of Athens against Persia, were willing to supply reinforcements. But not for ten days, however. "It would be sacrilege for us to go to war during the time of the Carneian festival," the Spartans told the Athenian courier. "We cannot march until after the full moon ten days hence."

Athens could not wait. By the time Pheidippides returned

with the bad news, the Persians were virtually at Athens' front door.

The Persian fleet had landed in the bay of Marathon, little more than 20 miles from Athens, and Datis' armies were assembling on the shore, where a level plain five miles long and two miles wide gave them ample room to maneuver. The Athenians hurriedly sent an army to prevent the Persians from moving inland.

The Athenian army numbered about 9,000 men. Ten generals led it, one of them Miltiades, a native of Athens who had spent many years in Persia and understood the Persians well. Each of the ten generals had equal authority, and above them was the polemarch, or war ruler, who that year was an Athenian noble named Callimachus.

The Athenians hoped to be able to block the Persians for the next two weeks. That would give Sparta time to finish its religious festival and send reinforcements. The Greeks under Callimachus and the ten generals took up a position in the valley of Avlona, overlooking the plain of Marathon. There, a thousand soldiers from the city of Plataea joined them.

For eight days the Persians on the plain and the Greeks in the mountain pass confronted each other without moving. Neither side dared to begin hostilities. The Athenians and Plataeans felt that they were not strong enough to deal with the Persians themselves, and had best wait for the arrival of the Spartan troops. The Persians, seeing the mountain passes blocked by Greek troops, decided to wait until Artaphernes had finished sacking Eretria, and then attack Athens by sea.

On the ninth day, word came of the fall of Eretria by treachery. Now alarm swept the Greek camp. The ten worried generals conferred.

"I say attack," Miltiades declared. "Attack immediately. If we wait any longer, Artaphernes will be upon us."

Four of the generals agreed with Miltiades. The other five

were reluctant to fight. "Let us wait," one of them said. "Soon the Spartans will send reinforcements to us. We are not strong enough to deal with the Persians alone."

"But if we wait for the Spartans," Miltiades countered, "Athens may be in ruins before they reach us."

With the general staff evenly divided, Callimachus, the polemarch, cast the deciding vote—to attack now, without waiting for the Spartan reinforcements. The risks were great. If their attack failed, and the Persians were triumphant, Athens would be looted and the hated Hippias restored to power. On the other hand, further delay might mean the destruction of Athens anyway, once Artaphernes' force joined that of Datis.

On September 21, 490, the Athenians, with their thousand allies from Plataea, drew up their battle formation. Miltiades was the general in command. He arrayed his 10,000 men in two columns, each half a mile long, and marched down toward the plain of Marathon. A much greater Persian force awaited them there.

The Greeks were armed with javelins and swords. They had no cavalry, no bowmen. The Persians were confident of success as they watched the approach of this skimpily outfitted army of citizen-soldiers. They feared nothing, those Persians. Weren't they the masters of the world? Didn't Persian nobles rule in Egypt and Babylon and even India? These Greeks were nuisances, nothing more. They would soon be swept to defeat.

All Greece was staked on the outcome of this battle. If the Athenians lost, it meant Greece would become a Persian dependency, since Sparta alone could not withstand the might of Darius. The newly kindled spark of democracy would be snuffed out, and Persian satraps in flowing robes would reign in the cities of Greece.

Less than a mile separated the two armies. Callimachus led the right wing of the Greeks. The Plataeans were on the left.

Two important Athenian generals, Themistocles and Aristides, commanded the center. Miltiades directed overall strategy.

The normal Greek war maneuver was to bring heavily armed spearmen forward in a solid line. But Miltiades chose to go to battle with his troops thinnest in the center, strongest on the flanks. He hoped that the center troops, though numerically weak, would hold their position while the right and left flanks moved in from the sides to enfold the Persians.

The cry of battle was given, and the Athenians rushed forward. Among the soldiers in the ranks was the great poet Aeschylus, in whose play *The Persians* the Greek war cry is preserved:

"On, sons of the Greeks! Strike for the freedom of your country! Strike for the freedom of your children and of your wives—for the shrines of your fathers' gods, and for the sepulchres of your fathers. All—all are now staked upon the strife!"

On the Greeks came, moving at a running pace over the mile of level ground that lay between the foot of the mountains and the Persian force. "When the Persians saw the Athenians running down on them," Herodotus wrote, "without horse or bowmen, and scanty in numbers, they thought them a set of madmen rushing to certain destruction."

The Persians were bewildered by the suicidal audacity of the Greek charge. Hastily, Datis' archers fitted arrows to their bows, and the Persian cavalry saddled up. A shower of arrows fell on the Greek line, but their bronze armor and their shields protected them, and they rushed into the Persian line. Soon the Greeks were so close that the Persians had no room to use their arrows effectively. The Persians had always relied on strength of numbers and the accuracy of their bowmen. They wore only light armor and wicker shields.

It was a story that was to be repeated many times in history: a small, determined, well-drilled army of men defending their homeland wreaking havoc on a larger but less well-organized force of invaders. Men who fight on their home ground have an advantage over invaders. The Athenians were fighting to defend their homes; the Persians were fighting simply for the glory of Darius. It was all the difference in the world, so far as morale went.

The weak center of the Greek line yielded under the thrust of the Persians. The troops under Themistocles and Aristides were forced back under the Persian charge, and were chased up valley toward the inner country. But as the Persians broke through the center, the Greeks brought their two wings down on them. The right wing under Callimachus, the left of Plataeans, wheeled inward to buffet the Persians.

The Persians fought bravely, but they had been out-maneuvered. The spears of the Greeks worked vigorously, and the troops of Darius fell by the hundreds. Desperately, the foremost Persians tried to hack their way through the Greek line, but the Greeks held fast, fighting fiercely now that they scented victory.

Toward evening, the Persians panicked. They were completely enfolded by the Greeks now and the slaughter was frightful. All thought of the glory of Darius forgotten, the Persians turned their backs and fled to the sea.

The jubilant Greeks gave pursuit. As the Persians hastily scrambled aboard their galleys and put out to sea, the Greek spears continued to take their toll. "Bring fire," the Greeks cried. "Burn their ships!"

Seven ships fell into Greek hands. The battle at the beach was a hectic one, and here the polemarch Callimachus died, and the brother of the poet Aeschylus.

The Persians under Datis fled. Datis still had hopes of attacking Athens by sea, and the remnants of the Persian armada sailed to the western coast of Greece to launch an attack on Athens. But Miltiades had guessed that this was

Datis' plan and, quickly leaving the battlefield, he marched his army overland back to Athens, where they awaited the arrival of the Persians. When Datis and his fleet entered the harbor of Athens, they saw the troops of Miltiades in full battle array on the heights above the city. Unwilling to risk a second defeat, the baffled Persians withdrew, and sailed eastward to lick their wounds.

The victory at Marathon had been as glorious as it was unexpected. The Persians had lost 6,400 men, but only 192 Athenians and a handful of the Plataeans had perished.

The promised Spartan reinforcements made their appearance on the evening of the battle. They had marched from Sparta in an amazing three days, but were too late to help the valiant Athenians. They marched to the battlefield to view the Persian dead, and then, praising the Athenians, they returned to their native city.

The battle of Marathon has added a word to our language. For when Datis and his army fled, Miltiades dispatched a courier to Athens to bring the good news of victory. The courier ran the whole distance—22 miles, 1,470 yards—in one long breathless spurt. Since his time, a "marathon" has come to mean any test of human endurance, and "marathon races" covering the same distance the courier ran are held in many cities every year throughout the world.

Some historical sources state that the name of the original "marathon" runner was Pheidippides. Other sources state Pheidippides was a courier who had been sent earlier to Sparta to ask for aid, and that the name of the runner who brought the victory news remains unknown.

The battle of Marathon did not end the Persian threat to Greece. It was not until another decade that Greece would securely establish its freedom from Persian menace. Darius died, and Xerxes took his place, and at the battle of Salamis, in 480 B.C., the Greek fleet destroyed Xerxes' forces while the great king himself watched the catastrophe from a nearby hillside. The following year, at the battle of Plataea, the Persian threat was ended decisively.

There are those who insist that Salamis, and not Marathon, was the decisive battle of the war between the Greeks and the Persians. I feel that the earlier battle is the greater one, even though the defeat handed the Persians at Salamis was far more costly in terms of lives lost.

Marathon was the first victory of the Athenians over the Persians. It had a symbolic value much greater than its actual military importance, both for the Athenians and for the Persians.

The Persians learned, to their dismay, that they were not invincible. The Athenians learned a much more inspiring lesson: that they were capable of defending their homeland, that they could outfight the invaders who would impose despotic rule on them. As General Fuller wrote in his account of the battle, "For the first time in their history the Greeks had beaten the Persians on their own element, the land, and Marathon endowed the victors with a faith in their destiny which was to endure for three centuries, during which western culture was born. Marathon was the birth cry of Europe."

Had the Athenians been defeated at Marathon, the idea of democracy would have been snuffed out virtually at its birth, and the course of world history would have been unimaginably different. The arrogant Persians, buoyed by a victory over Greece, might well have gone on to conquer all of Europe, and there would have been no Roman Empire, no world as we know it today.

Marathon—followed by Salamis and Plataea—shattered the self-confidence of the Persians, and their empire began to totter. Captive peoples in every part of the Persian Empire, inspired by the success of the Athenians, rebelled against the Persians. The myth of Persian invincibility was exploded.

From the day of Marathon on, the power of Persia declined.

The story of Greece after Marathon is a splendid one, but darkened by tragedy. Athens went on to its glorious golden age, the era of Sophocles and Pericles, of Thucydides, Plato, Socrates. But strife between the cities of Greece brought this age of wonders to a brutal end. Sparta warred on Athens and subjugated her, and from then on Greece had no importance as a political power, though she was the center of all philosophy and science for many hundreds of years afterward, and her great thinkers had enormous effect in shaping the world that was to come.

A century and a half after Marathon, a conqueror came from the rude country of Macedon, to the north of Athens. Alexander the Great—educated by Greeks, a Greek in all but birth—subdued the strife-ridden cities of Greece and then turned his attention to the rest of the world. At the battle of Arbela, in 331 B.C., Alexander smashed the Persian power for good, and made Persia part of the Macedonian Empire.

Alexander's empire was short-lived. It collapsed when he died, and Seleucus I, one of his generals, became the ruler of Persia. From then on, Persia, with its Macedonian and Greek rulers, remained an important country, but no longer the leading power of the world.

Power was passing. Two new forces were entering the international scene. One was destined to dominate all the known world for centuries, the other to have a brief moment of power, then to taste defeat. The rivalry between these two peoples was heightened by the fact that they both had a common ancestry.

Virgil's *Aeneid* tells of the fate of the city of Troy after the Greeks had conquered it. Virgil's hero is Aeneas, the son of Anchises. Aeneas leads a band of survivors out of Troy, and they go first from Troy, which was in Asia Minor, to the north coast of Africa. Here, the seafaring Phoenicians had established a colony called Carthage, meaning "New Town." Virgil tells of Aeneas' brief romance with the Carthaginian queen Dido, and then of Aeneas' abrupt and rather ungallant departure for Italy.

In Italy, Aeneas and his band of Trojans settled in a region called Latium, where he married the daughter of a local king and founded a city. Many years later, descendants of this union founded another city—Rome.

All this is legend, of course. Virgil's tale is an exciting one, but there may be little real truth in it. We do know, though, that about the year 1000 B.C., the Phoenicians established the city of Carthage in North Africa, while another wandering group of Asiatic people began to settle in what is now Italy.

During the years of conflict between Greece and Persia, Rome and Carthage quietly grew. A group of villages merged to become the city of Rome, and then Rome spread out, conquering the native peoples of the Italian peninsula and achieving sway throughout most of Italy. And during the same years the seafaring merchants of Carthage roved the Mediterranean, and Carthage become a wealthy city.

By 295 B.C., Rome was the master of all Italy, except for a few Greek colony cities on the southern coast and in Sicily. One by one, these cities fell to Rome. Rome was now the leading military power in Europe, and Carthage was the leading naval power. The two new giants faced each other uncomfortably across the Mediterranean. Conflict between them was inevitable.

The first serious dispute between Rome and Carthage arose over the Greek colony of Sicily, which was under Carthaginian influence and which Rome coveted. In 264 B.C., war broke out between Rome and Carthage over Sicily.

Seeing that they could not hope to defeat Carthage unless they became a naval power, the Romans boldly built a fleet.

At first they were repulsed by the far more experienced Carthaginians. But the incredible Roman persistence and discipline won out. They defeated Carthage at sea and became mighty at sea, with a fleet of 330 ships.

But a terrible storm, in 255 B.C., wiped out nearly all of the Roman fleet, and restored the supremacy of Carthage. And so the war seesawed on. A second storm, in 249 B.C., wrecked the rebuilt Roman fleet, and left Rome discouraged and weak. And the brilliant campaigns of a Carthaginian general named Hamilcar Barca kept Sicily from falling into Roman hands.

The indefatigable Romans wore Carthage out. They built a new fleet in 242 B.C., took the Carthaginians by surprise, and scored a resounding victory. Exhausted by more than two decades of continual war, Carthage sued for peace, and Sicily became a Roman province. A few years later, Rome was able to take advantage of Carthage's continued weakness to seize the island of Sardinia.

Rome now left Carthage in peace and turned in other directions—for the idea of world dominion, which had infected the Assyrians, and then the Persians, and then Alexander's Macedonians, now inflamed Rome. Between 229 and 219 B.C. the Romans waged war against the barbaric Gauls to the north, and extended their rule upward into Europe.

Carthage recovered her strength during those years, and under Hamilcar Barca conquered Spain. Carthage now held control of the western end of the Mediterranean, and again threatened the expansion of Rome's power.

A new war between Rome and Carthage became inevitable. Hamilcar Barca was dead, but his sons Hannibal and Hasdrubal had taken his place.

The moment of conflict came. Carthage vowed to shatter the might of Rome. The stakes in the war were enormous, the outcome uncertain.

CHAPTER
TWO

THE BATTLE OF ZAMA
The Downfall of Hannibal

EIGHTY dull-gray elephants formed the front line of the enemy army confronting the legions of Rome. Massive, ponderous, the huge beasts lashed their trunks through the air as they awaited the order to charge the foe. It was an array calculated to strike terror into any army—even the mighty warriors of Rome!

The year was 202 B.C. The rising power of Rome stood massed against the forces of her great rival, the city of Carthage in North Africa. For more than 60 years, Rome and Carthage had been fighting a desperate struggle. The prize to the winner was world power; the share of the loser, destruction and oblivion.

The war had gone with Rome. Carthage had been driven back, yielding its empire bit by agonizing bit to the onrushing Romans. The Roman military skill had proven unsurpassable.

And Rome had the confident conviction that destiny was on her side.

But one man arose to block the Roman dream of world conquest. He was the great Carthaginian general, Hannibal, who took command of the armies of Carthage in 218 B.C. Hannibal was a military genius who kept tottering Carthage from disaster and brought the cold chill of fear to Roman hearts. For 16 years Hannibal out-generaled the Romans— until the Battle of Zama.

He was a crafty man. He had spies lurking everywhere, bringing him news from Rome often before the Roman armies had received it. He wore disguises himself to go on spying missions from time to time. He was worshiped by his soldiers. His word was law.

The Roman historian Dio Cassius wrote of him, "He could lower the superb, elevate the humble, inspire here terror, there confidence; all this in a moment whenever he chose." The great historian Livy said, "His fearlessness in encountering dangers, and his prudence when in the midst of them, were extreme."

The great weapons of the one-eyed Hannibal were three in number: his wild, spirited, fighting men; his wonderful strategic skill; and his force of enormous, terrifying, trained war elephants. In 218 B.C., Hannibal launched an army from Spain, just across the Mediterranean from Carthage, and drove eastward through what is now France and was then called Gaul. He crossed the Alps with his elephants and struck deep into Italy. Though his armies suffered heavily, they annihilated the Romans at every battle.

The Roman generals were stunned by Hannibal's successes. "His soldiers are only barbarians," they exclaimed in bewilderment. "They are scarcely trained. They fight like wild men. And yet they defeat us!"

Rome's soldiers were indeed better trained in the arts of

war. But no Roman general had the insight, the daring, the sparkling brilliance of Hannibal. He knew how to outguess, how to outfeint, how to outmaneuver. He smashed every Roman army that came against him, and took firm possession of much of southern Italy. All that remained was for him to march on Rome and take the city. The upstart Roman nation would be vanquished at last.

Hannibal never took his opportunity. He might have marched in 216, after shattering the Roman forces at Cannae. His cavalry general, Maharbal, urged him vigorously: "Now is the time to march on Rome, Hannibal! The city will be yours."

Hannibal refused to march. The infuriated Maharbal cried, "Of a truth the gods have not bestowed all things upon the same person. You know how to conquer, Hannibal; but you do not know how to make use of your victory."

History would have been vastly different if Hannibal had captured Rome in 216 B.C. But he felt that Rome was too strong. He did not have the ships to blockade Rome by sea, nor the troops to lay siege effectively by land. He decided instead to encircle Rome by capturing her colonies in Spain, Sardinia and Sicily, and by winning the walled cities of Italy that paid tribute to Rome. Hannibal switched from the offensive to the defensive after he had captured the territory surrounding Rome. He concentrated on keeping his gains in Italy and hoping that Rome would weaken in time.

Rome did not weaken. But neither did Rome attempt to drive Hannibal out of Italy. The stalemated war dragged on and on, Hannibal holding to his captured land and Rome making only a token attempt to dislodge him. Rome's leading general, Fabius, was called "Cunctator," the "Delayer," because he held back and refused to make a direct assault against Hannibal.

But new Roman generals arose who resolved to crush Carthage. One of them, Scipio, drove the Carthaginians out of Spain. At the battle of the Metaurus, in 207 B.C., Hannibal's brother Hasdrubal was routed and his severed head sent contemptuously to Hannibal by the Romans. Hannibal himself remained in the "boot of Italy, too strong to be driven out but not strong enough to extend his conquests to Rome herself.

While Hannibal held tight in southern Italy, Scipio took the offensive across the Mediterranean into Africa, virtually to Carthage's own doorstep. With Scipio's armies almost at the city walls, the Carthaginians panicked and sent for Hannibal, telling him to come back from Italy to defend the homeland.

Hannibal was not willing to give up his hard-won position in Italy. But Carthage herself was in danger. Indeed, before Hannibal could set sail for Rome, Carthage was forced to beg for peace. Scipio's armies surrounded the city and a peace treaty was being negotiated with the Romans when electrifying news reached Carthage.

"Hannibal has landed! Hannibal is on his way to save us!"

With an army of 20,000 men, Hannibal had landed on African shores. Immediately the jubilant Carthaginians broke off the peace talks and treacherously imprisoned the Roman envoys. Scipio and the Roman soldiers were taken by surprise and found themselves in a ticklish spot. They were on hostile soil, far from home, with the enemy's most dreaded general approaching. To make things worse for the Romans, Scipio did not even have his full army with him for, during the peace talks, he had sent some of his troops to go to the aid of an ally of Rome nearby, Masinissa, King of Numidia.

In this tight spot Scipio chose the path of boldness. He knew that sooner or later he would have to face the invincible Hannibal, and he did not want to do it near Carthage, where Hannibal would easily be able to obtain reinforcements and supplies. Calling his generals together, Scipio declared, "We will move inland and force Hannibal to follow us."

The Roman legions set out for the valley of the Bagradas, a rich, fertile area that produced much of Carthage's food and grain. As they passed through the farmlands the Romans burned, plundered, looted, destroying Hannibal's supply lines. In order to put a stop to this destruction, Hannibal found himself compelled to leave the security of his base at Carthage and follow Scipio into the interior to defeat him there.

Hannibal struck camp and set out after Scipio. He marched toward the town of Zama, five days' march southwest of Carthage. But before his armies could encounter those of Scipio, bad news for Carthage arrived:

"Masinissa has joined Scipio!" a breathless messenger cried. "He has come with 6,000 infantrymen and 4,000 cavalry!"

Hannibal was dismayed. His own army numbered about 50,000, as against only 36,000 for the combined forces of Scipio and Masinissa. But the Roman soldiers were far more capable, man for man, and their cavalry would far outnumber Hannibal's now.

For the first time in his 16-year career as Carthage's general, Hannibal saw possible defeat. Under the blazing African sun he went out now to parley with Scipio as the opposing forces arrayed themselves at the town of Zama.

The two commanders, accompanied only by interpreters, met in the open space between the two armies. Hannibal offered a treaty in which Carthage would relinquish all claim to Sicily, Sardinia, and Spain.

But Scipio had already had one taste of Carthaginian treachery in treaty-signing, and he was wary. Besides, he felt that his forces were stronger than Hannibal's. So he haughtily brushed aside Hannibal's proposal. "I cannot again trust the word of a Carthaginian," he declared.

"Then we must do battle," Hannibal said.

"If we must, we shall," Scipio answered. "The attack will commence at dawn."

Hannibal knew all too well how weak his army was, despite its size. He had three infantry groups: his own tried and true men, veterans of his many Italian campaigns; the troops of his other brother, Mago, who had just died; and a hastily assembled force of new recruits.

Hannibal put Mago's men in the front line. They were not Carthaginians, but tough, well-trained men from Gaul and Liguria (western Italy). Right behind them, he assembled the large force of inexperienced recruits. And in the third line, 200 yards to the rear of the second, he arrayed his own battle-hardened Carthaginians.

In his past battles with the Romans, Hannibal had had strong cavalry divisions that he had used to outflank the enemy. At his great victory of Cannae he had sent his cavalry around to attack the Romans from the rear, causing great devastation. But at Zama he had only 2,000 cavalry; Scipio at least three times as many. There could be no outflanking today. Hannibal could hope for success only by a direct head-on attack. He put a thousand Carthaginian cavalry on the right wing, a thousand Numidians on the left, to serve as shields for his infantry.

His most spectacular force consisted of 80 elephants—more than he had ever used in one battle before. Hannibal placed the great beasts along the front line, in front of Mago's Ligurian and Gallic soldiers. His strategy was simple. The charging elephants, Hannibal hoped, would throw the Romans into confusion and disorder. Mago's experienced troops would break through the Roman lines, scattering them. Then the second wave, the game but inexperienced new recruits, would charge in, making up in number what they lacked in skill. And finally, with the Romans in disarray, Hannibal's own picked troops of the third line would swoop in for the *coup de grâce*.

On the other side of the field, Scipio was using the traditional Roman battle formation with some special adaptations to suit the situation. His troops were of four types: *hastati* (javelin throwers); *principes* (spearmen); *triarii* (veteran spearmen) and *velites* (light infantry). The usual arrangement was to place the *hastati* in the first line, the *principes* in the second, and the *triarii* in the third, using the *velites* as flankers. This Scipio did. But instead of arranging his men in alternating checkerboard fashion from row to row to present a solid front, Scipio left wide aisles through which he planned to let the Carthaginian elephants pass. Also, he drew the *triarii* farther back than usual, to give them room to cope with the rampaging elephants. On his left flank, Scipio placed his own cavalry, under Laelius; on the right wing, he put Masinissa's Numidian force, both infantry and cavalry.

Hannibal gave the order for the elephants to charge. Eighty gigantic "living tanks" thundered toward the waiting Romans as the battle began. Dust rose high. But Scipio had a surprise planned. The men in his front line suddenly whipped out trumpets! A terrifying clamor split the air!

The shrill trumpet calls terrified the elephants. In fright, the unwieldy beasts turned back. Only a few continued on, smashing through and doing great damage among Scipio's troops. But most of the elephants charged Hannibal's own lines in their bewilderment. Spurred on by the shrieking trumpets, the panicky animals hurtled into Hannibal's left wing of cavalry just as the horsemen were about to attack. The cavalry was thrown into confusion, and Masinissa and his Numidians took advantage of the crisis to charge in, driving Hannibal's entire left cavalry wing from the field.

The same thing was happening on the right. There, the Roman cavalry under Laelius was routing Hannibal's other cavalry wing and driving it, too, into retreat.

Those elephants that had not turned back against Hannibal plowed forward. But Scipio's cunningly devised aisles now opened wide, and the elephants continued on, passing harm-lessly through the Roman legions and on into the open fields beyond. Hannibal now found himself at the outset of the battle stripped of his cavalry and his elephants both—thanks to Scipio's idea of using trumpets to frighten the mighty beasts.

The first phase of the battle was over. Now, as the sun rose blisteringly in the cloudless blue sky, a brutal frontal attack started. The front lines of both armies collided with a ringing clang of shields. The veteran Ligurians and Gauls that Mago had trained performed valiantly, and for a while held the upper hand.

But as each front-line Roman fell, another stepped forward to take his place. On the Carthaginian side it was otherwise. The untrained recruits of Hannibal's second line held back in fear. Slowly, the ranks of Mago's men were thinned. The Carthaginian front line was forced steadily back.

"Where's the second line?" Mago's men asked each other in the heat of the battle. "Why aren't they supporting us?"

"They're afraid!" someone shouted. "They aren't going to fight!"

Sudden panic swept the Carthaginian front line. Feeling that they had been betrayed by the men behind them, they turned to flee. But now, the hesitant second line closed ranks against their own allies. Under orders to hold their formation no matter what, they refused to let the feeling Gauls and Ligurians break through. A battle broke out between Han-nibal's own first and second lines, while the gleeful Romans completed their massacre of Hannibal's front-line men.

Belatedly the second line showed heroism. Now that the soldiers of Mago's army were gone, the raw recruits of the second line had to bear the brunt of Scipio's assault. They rose to the challenge, holding off the *hastati*, or javelin wielders.

The ground was covered with corpses and was slippery with blood.

The Romans, who had scented victory half an hour before, were troubled by this unexpected display of valor on the part of Hannibal's unskilled second line. The *hastati* wavered, and their tight formation began to break up as fallen corpses interfered with their positions. "When they had surmounted the obstacles," wrote the historian Polybius, "the two lines charged each other with the greatest fire and fury. Being nearly equal in spirit, numbers, courage, and arms, the battle was for a long time undecided, the men in their obstinate valor falling dead without giving way a step."

During all this, Hannibal kept his third line back, out of the fray. They were his most experienced soldiers, and he was saving them. He did not believe in sending a line into battle while the line in front was still unbroken.

The *hastati* and the *principes* surged forward, and even the *triarii*, Scipio's third line, entered the fray. The Carthaginian second line gave way steadily, and finally broke into flight.

Now the battle entered its final stage. In the words of Livy, the Romans "had penetrated to their real antagonists, men equal to them in the nature of their arms, in their experience of war, in the fame of their achievements."

The advantage now appeared to lie with Hannibal. He still had the nucleus of his army intact—24,000 superb fighting men, skilled in battle, and completely fresh and rested. Against them, Scipio could only throw some 20,000 men, many of them already weary from the struggle against Hannibal's second line.

Once again Scipio showed his bold inventive nature. He called his troops together and, with the enemy only a few hundred yards away, completely rearranged his forces. Instead of a wide frontage that overlapped the Carthaginian line, he now drew his *hastati* together in a concentrated unit that was as solid as possible. He sent the *principes* and *triarii* out on the flanks to reinforce the front line, stringing them out on a wide arc.

Scipio's idea was to smash powerfully into the Carthaginian lines with his massed *hastati*, and then to encircle the enemy with the *principes* and *triarii*. This, he hoped, would put Hannibal's army in a position where it could be easily attacked when the cavalry under Masinissa and Laelius returned from its pursuit of Hannibal's horsemen.

Masinissa and Laelius, though, had apparently been too energetic in their chase, and had gone far from the battlefield. Scipio was compelled to fight a delaying action until they returned. His tired men struggled doggedly against Hannibal's rested veterans, and the issue hung in doubt as the long day waned and the sun began to slip toward the horizon.

Then, in the literal nick of time, the Roman cavalry appeared. The horsemen charged the rear of Hannibal's army. Hannibal's infantry, pinned by foot soldiers in front, cavalry behind, was cut to pieces. The battle ended in a rout. The Roman cries of victory were loud. The Carthaginians fought virtually to the last man. When all was clearly lost, Hannibal and a few of his aides made their escape.

Scipio now turned toward Carthage. Capture of Carthage itself was out of the question; the city was magnificently fortified, and Scipio's decimated army was in no condition to mount a prolonged siege. Scipio offered peace terms to Carthage, and the war-weary city, at Hannibal's advice, accepted. Under the terms of peace, Carthage agreed to pay Rome a tribute of 10,000 talents of silver (some $15,000,000) over the next 50 years, to hand all its warships and elephants over to Rome, and to carry on no future war without Rome's consent.

Hannibal was chosen by his defeated people to head the

government of Carthage, and ruled wisely until 196 B.C., when he was compelled by Roman schemes to flee into exile. For the next 13 years he lived abroad, planning campaigns against Rome that were never carried out, and fighting the battles of other kings. In 183 B.C., a cowardly king who had hired Hannibal as a general agreed to turn him over to the Romans. But the noble Carthaginian cheated his lifelong enemies by taking poison before they could seize him.

The Battle of Zama is one of the great turning points in world history because it marked the end of Carthage's hopes of destroying the rising power of Rome. So long as Carthage had the brilliant Hannibal, there was the possibility of ultimate victory over Rome. At Zama, Hannibal tasted defeat for the first time, and Carthage never recovered.

And so Rome, which only a century before had been master merely of a small section of Italy, extended its sway to Spain, Sicily, North Africa, and the entire western Mediterranean area, without a challenger. The city of Carthage, the sole rival to Rome's sway, had been destroyed. For the next six hundred years—a time longer than that from Columbus' to our own—Rome would rule the world.

THE BATTLE OF ACTIUM

Octavian Wins a World

DURING the two centuries after the crushing of Carthage, Rome gradually extended her power throughout the known world. The Romans gobbled up the fragments of Alexander the Great's sundered empire, and in the process made themselves masters of Greece and Egypt—learning much of the wisdom of these older countries. With Carthage obliterated, North Africa became a Roman province. Roman armies ventured into the wild forests of western Europe to subdue the Gauls and other barbarian tribes.

While this outward expansion was going on, Rome went through the kind of internal political turmoil that any fast-growing empire must cope with. In the earliest days, Rome had been ruled by kings—but they had been overthrown, and a republic endured for centuries, ruled by consuls elected regularly, and by a senate of wealthy Romans.

Soon the consul-senate system was breaking down. The empire was becoming too unwieldy to be ruled by various elected officials. Strong central authority seemed called for.

In the first century before Christ, two powerful leaders, Sulla and Marius, contended for the right to rule Rome. Marius, when he ruled, still called himself consul. Sulla took the title of dictator, and bloodily purged Rome of his enemies. After Sulla's death, one of his officers, Pompey, rose to the fore. In 70 B.C., he was elected consul, and set about repealing Sulla's harsh laws. Then, for eight years he campaigned throughout the Roman dominions, crushing the last vestige of opposition to Roman rule. When he returned in triumph to Rome in 61 B.C., many Romans wished to make him absolute ruler, even give him a crown. The old Roman Republic was collapsing, and in the new climate of easygoing luxury and wealth it was generally felt that the time had come for Rome to have a king who would reign in pomp and splendor.

Pompey's rise to power was interrupted by the entry of a new political figure: Gaius Julius Caesar, a noble whose aunt had been the wife of the Consul Marius. Caesar and Pompey formed an alliance with a third leading Roman, Crassus. Under the agreement Caesar was to be elected consul, and Pompey and Crassus to rule important provinces.

Pompey obviously did not expect Caesar to become the powerful man he was to be. Caesar's victories against the Gauls, and his brilliant generalship, made him the man of the hour in Rome. As Caesar's power grew, Pompey turned against him. The Roman Senate supported Pompey—but Caesar had the backing of the people and of the army.

Civil war broke out. Pompey fled Italy. Caesar put a young associate, Mark Antony, in charge of the army in Italy, and himself led the pursuit of Pompey. After first defeating Pompey's forces in Spain, Caesar turned to Pompey himself, who was in Egypt. Combined forces under Caesar and Mark

Antony defeated Pompey, who was murdered by Egyptians after his downfall, in 48 B.C.

While in Egypt, Caesar had become romantically entangled with Cleopatra, the Egyptian queen, and it was not until 46 B.C. that he returned to Rome. Quelling the last vestige of opposition, Caesar accepted the rank of dictator for a ten-year term. But two years later, at the height of his triumph, his enemies assassinated him.

There were two chief contenders for the power Caesar had held. The first was Mark Antony, Caesar's loyal lieutenant; a romantic, dashing man. The other was Caesar's grand nephew and adopted son, Octavian, who was only nineteen when Caesar died. He fell heir to most of Caesar's estate, and appointed himself Caesar's avenger.

At first Antony and Octavian saw eye to eye. But then the important post of tribune fell vacant, and young Octavian applied to Antony for it. Antony refused him. Antony was afraid that the young man would be too zealous in prosecuting Caesar's slayers, which could lead to a new civil war. And he felt Octavian was too young for the job.

Octavian promptly set out to win support from the army, which had always been loyal to Caesar. With strong backing, Octavian rose to the rank of consul when he was barely twenty, and then offered to make peace with Antony.

Antony, Octavian, and a third Roman named Lepidus agreed to divide power among themselves. They formed a triumvirate, with Octavian being given the rule over Sicily, Sardinia, and Africa; Antony, of Gaul; and Lepidus, of Spain. Lepidus would also control the central government in Italy while Octavian and Antony made war on Caesar's murderers, Brutus and Cassius.

After the overthrow of the two assassins, in 42 B.C., there was peace in Rome for a short while. But the friction between Octavian and Antony grew. There was not room in one empire, no matter how large, for both of them. Lepidus was cast from power and Antony and Octavian began to carve up the provinces of Rome.

Antony had grandiose ideas of becoming a second Alexander the Great and of ruling in luxury over the Orient. He marched into the Near East in 36 B.C., but suffered a severe defeat at the hands of the ferocious Parthians, losing 30,000 men. While Octavian made himself the master of the western provinces, Antony wandered on through the east, reaching Egypt ultimately.

There he had his celebrated love affair with Cleopatra. He married her, named her "Queen of Kings," and planned to join Rome and the eastern kingdoms in one grand empire.

Octavian used this as a means of stirring up hatred toward Antony in Rome. "He has married the Egyptian queen," Octavian declared. "If he is successful, he will make Egypt his capital. Rome will become unimportant, a mere provincial city. He will give Rome to Cleopatra as her plaything!"

All Italy swore allegiance to Octavian in the face of this threat to Rome's dominance. In 33 B.C., Antony and Cleopatra began to assemble a fleet and an army with which to challenge Octavian for the mastery of the Roman Empire.

Octavian carried out a shrewd political move. Antony still had many friends in Rome—so Octavian arranged for war to be declared against Cleopatra, but not against Antony. This left Antony in an impossible position. If he invaded Italy, he would lose what remaining support he had, and would make himself an enemy of Rome. But if he did not fight at Cleopatra's side, he would arouse *her* enmity, and leave himself without an army.

Antony could do nothing but wait for the situation to change. And while he waited, Octavian mobilized his forces and moved eastward to wage war against Cleopatra.

It was 31 B.C. The rivalry between Antony and Octavian

was approaching its climax. To the victor would go unquestioned rule of the vast Roman Empire.

Antony had left Egypt with Cleopatra and had made his headquarters in Greece, where he sat hesitating, not knowing whether to return to Egypt or forge on to Rome. He and Cleopatra had assembled a major army in Greece—some 70,000 soldiers, and eight squadrons of 60 ships each. Some of these ships were enormous, with artillery turrets and ironbound timber shields as defense against ramming.

Octavian came down into Greece with an even greater force—an infantry of 80,000, a cavalry of 12,000 (Antony had a cavalry of the same size) and more than 400 ships, some of them armed with catapults that could fire the *harpax,* a kind of iron hook that caught enemy ships and held them for boarding. Octavian put his fleet under the command of his trusted general, Agrippa.

Agrippa's fleet made a sudden swoop that captured some of Antony's ships and cut his line of supply to Egypt. At the very outset, then, Antony was badly hampered. Food ran short. Many of his soldiers and even some of his generals, sensing defeat, deserted.

Canidius, one of Antony's advisers, suggested, "Let us abandon the fleet and withdraw into Macedonia, where we can fight in the open. We have no other chance."

"No," Cleopatra insisted. "The war will be decided at sea."

Privately Antony had lost all hope. But since he could not feed his army, he agreed with Cleopatra that they would have to rely on the fleet. Cleopatra, meanwhile, was secretly making preparations for her escape in case of defeat.

The odds against Antony were great. But he hoped for a miracle that would save him.

Octavian had taken a position near Actium, a jutting promontory in northern Greece. Antony's camp was on the south side of the strait of Preveza, two miles south of Actium.

Antony knew that on that coast in summer, the morning wind normally blew in from the sea, but in midday shifted direction and blew strongly northwest. "Antony knew," we read in the *Cambridge Ancient History*, "that when he came out he would find Octavian's fleet to seaward of him, and he meant to use the wind when it shifted to turn their left and drive them southward (down wind) away from their camp; were they broken or dispersed, he could starve the camp out. . . . But in case the battle miscarried he had a second plan, known only to Cleopatra and Canidius: they would break through to Egypt with what ships they could, and Canidius would bring the rest of the army back overland."

Octavian had been given word of Antony's first plan by deserters. "Let them break out of port," Octavian said. "When they're at sea, we'll attack from the rear and capture Antony and Cleopatra. The fleet will surrender once they're taken!"

Agrippa, a better general than his leader, disagreed. "They will outsail us and escape," he pointed out. "This way we have them trapped. Let's keep them penned up."

Octavian yielded. Instead of allowing Antony to escape and then giving chase, they would enter battle at once. Agrippa drew up his ships in a line of battle facing the strait and waited for Antony to emerge. It was September 2, 31 B.C. Some 400 ships were numbered in each of the opposing fleets.

When the wind calmed, Antony came out, and waited for the change in wind direction. His fleet was divided into three wings—the right wing, 170 ships, under his own command; the center, 60 ships, under Marcus Octavius; and the left, 120 ships, under C. Sosius. Backing up this line were 60 ships under Cleopatra's command. This rear line had a double purpose. First, Cleopatra would serve to prevent ships of the front line from retreating or deserting. Secondly, Antony planned that the change of wind would veer Octavian's left wing, and when that happened, he would move outward to attack, and

Cleopatra's squadron would move up to fill the gap in his line.

Octavian also knew all about the change of wind. And his plan was to turn Antony's right wing, which of course faced his own left wing. Octavian had his ships deployed in three groups, the left under Agrippa, the center under Arruntius, and the right under his own command.

At noon the wind shifted. Both Antony and Agrippa hurried to take advantage of it. Antony's right wing drew outward to meet Octavian's left wing, under Agrippa. It does not seem that Antony was fighting simply to break through and escape. He was fighting to win, to crush Octavian's navy.

Agrippa's ships were lighter than Antony's. But what they lacked in strength, they made up for in agility. Naval battle at that time consisted of trying to sink the enemy's ships by ramming them with your own, and if failing that, to grapple the ship, board it, and overcome its crew. The historian Dio Cassius, writing several centuries after the battle, remarked that if Agrippa's ships did not succeed in sinking a rammed enemy, "they would backwater before coming to grips, and would either ram the same vessels suddenly again, or would let those go and turn their attention to others. . . . The enemy, on the other hand, tried to hit the approaching ships with dense showers of stones and arrows, and to cast iron grapnels upon their assailants."

The quiet waters of the strait churned as the milling ships fought for advantage. Dio Cassius tells us:

"On the one side the pilots and the rowers endured the most hardship and fatigue, and on the other side the marines; and the one side resembled cavalry, now making a charge and now retreating, since it was in their power to attack and back off at will, and the others were like heavy armed troops guarding against the approach of foes and trying their best to hold them. Consequently each gained advantages over the other; the one party would run in upon the lines of oars projecting from the ships and shatter the blades, and the other party, fighting from the higher level, would sink them with stones and engines."

This fierce phase of the battle saw the two fleets at equal strength. But then what Antony had feared most began to happen: his ships began to desert. The 180 ships of the center and left wings abruptly backwatered and headed for shore in dismal retreat. The two leftmost squadrons of his own wing would have done the same, except that they were blocked from behind by Cleopatra's squadron. Unable to flee, they meekly raised their oars as a sign of surrender.

Scowling, Antony roared to his lieutenants, "There's nothing for us to do but fight all the harder!" But now victory was hopeless. They had to fight to escape.

Cleopatra chose to flee. She hoisted the purple sails of her flagship, the *Antonia*, and made for the open sea accompanied by the rest of her squadron. Seeing this, Antony's remaining ships determined to flee as well. They began to dump their artillery turrets and engines of war into the sea, lightening themselves for flight. In Dio's words:

"While they were occupied in this way their adversaries fell upon them; they had not pursued the fugitives, because they themselves were without sails and were prepared only for a naval battle, and there were many to fight against each ship, both from afar and alongside. Therefore on both sides alike the conflict took on the greatest variety and was waged with the utmost bitterness. For the men of Caesar [Octavian] damaged the lower parts of the ships all around, crushed the oars, snapped off the rudders, and climbed on the decks, seized hold of some of the foe and pulled them down, pushed off others, fought with yet others, since they were not equal to them in numbers.

"And Antony's men pushed their assailants back with boat-hooks, cut them down with axes, hurled down upon them stones and heavy missiles made ready for just this purpose, drove back those who tried to climb up, and fought with those who came within reach."

Antony's men, fighting for their lives, resisted stubbornly. The fleet of Octavian took a new approach to the battle. Writes Dio: "And now another kind of battle was entered upon. The assailants would approach their victims from many directions at once, shoot blazing missiles at them, hurl with their hands torches fastened to javelins, and with the aid of engines would throw from a distance pots full of charcoal and pitch."

Antony's own flagship was caught by grapnels. He escaped to another ship, and, leading 40 of his vessels, managed to elude Octavian's attackers and slip out to sea, where he joined Cleopatra. Together they fled. Antony, furious with Cleopatra for having deserted him, would not speak to her for three days. The battle of Actium had ended in rout, in catastrophe for Antony.

Octavian and Agrippa, in the confusion of the victory, did not attempt to pursue the escaped Antony and Cleopatra. Since Octavian's ships had no sails, merely oars, it would have been difficult to give chase. He contented himself with capturing and burning the 300 ships that had deserted Antony. Antony's crew, and the soldiers on land under Canidius, surrendered and joined Octavian's army.

Antony's power was broken. The following summer Octavian invaded Egypt, and Antony's remaining troops deserted to the enemy as soon as they learned of Octavian's approach. Antony, hearing a rumor that Cleopatra had committed suicide, stabbed himself. Cleopatra still lived—but rather than fall into Octavian's hands she clasped a poisonous asp to her bosom, and died of its bite. For 22 years this beautiful, unscrupulous queen had manipulated the rulers of Rome, but no more.

Octavian was the supreme ruler of Rome. At Actium he had won a world. In the name of the Roman people, he annexed Egypt, and returned in triumph to Rome. In 27 B.C., he received the title of *Augustus*, or "Majestic," from the Roman Senate, and was named Imperator—Emperor—for a period of 10 years. His term of office was renewed again and again, and his rule was ended only by his death, in 14 A.D., after he had ruled as the first emperor of Rome for more than 40 years.

Caesar Augustus—to use the name by which he was known after becoming emperor—is perhaps the most towering single figure in all of Roman history, and it was at Actium that he achieved his full power. By the end of his reign, Rome was undisputed master of the world from the British Isles to the Orient, and Augustus was the undisputed master of Rome. His reign was a time of serenity, of strength. He had replaced the tottering fabric of the Roman Republic with the newer and stronger bonds of the Roman Empire.

What if Antony had won at Actium? If Cleopatra had not panicked, if Antony's ships had held firm, if Octavian had fallen?

History would be vastly different. No doubt Antony would have proceeded to Rome in triumph. But Antony was not the same manner of man as Augustus. Antony was weak, self-seeking. He could never have wielded power as Augustus did, nor forged an empire so sturdy. Within a generation, perhaps, Rome would have collapsed into a host of warring provinces. There would have been no central authority to provide stability and sanity for the world for the next several centuries.

All that was the work of Augustus. He matured into a great statesman, and the empire that he built—for all the faults of his successors—was a monument to his wisdom and ability. The soldiers of Rome carried civilization to the farthest reaches of the known world. They spread that rule of law and order that is the foundation of our modern society. And all the work of Augustus would never have been carried out, had the luck of that charming weakling Antony been better, that September day at Actium.

CHAPTER

FOUR

THE BATTLE OF ADRIANOPLE

An Empire Falls

WHEN did Rome fall?

We can argue about it for days. Some people would say that Rome fell in 1453 A.D., when the Moslem armies captured Constantinople. But the Roman Empire that fell in that year was not the empire of the Caesars, but a second empire, a Christian empire far from Italy. 1453 saw the fall of new Rome. The real Roman Empire had fallen long before.

There are those who would put the fall of Rome at 476 A.D. In that year Romulus Augustulus, the last of the Caesars, surrendered to the barbarians. Certainly that was when Rome fell.

But no, that was the *coup de grâce*, the final stroke. Rome had been falling for a long while earlier. Since 455, perhaps, when Valentinian III, last of the great emperors, was murdered; or since 429, when the Vandals took Africa away from

Rome. A number of significant events have been named as the fall of Rome, and each has its own claim.

My own feeling is that Rome received its deathblow in 378 A.D. The empire had been in a bad way before that year, but not so bad that a single strong leader of the caliber of Augustus could not have saved the situation. But in 378 the battle of Adrianople was fought—and after that the decline of Rome became irreversible. Rome received a mortal wound at Adrianople, though she was a long time dying.

Rome, for all its might, had been plagued by the barbarians of Europe for centuries. As early as 390 B.C. the Gauls had entered the confines of the city of Rome itself, and had nearly forced the city to her knees in a seven-month siege before they were driven off. Even in Rome's greatest years, it was necessary to maintain constant vigilance against barbarian marauders who showed no fear of the glittering city on the Tiber.

In the first three centuries after Christ, the job of holding off the barbarians became more and more taxing as the military prowess of Rome declined. The Romans, pleasure-loving, wallowing in luxuries, had lost the stern discipline that had won them their empire. Again and again the barbarians prodded Rome's borders.

The new marauders were called the Goths. They were a wandering people that had come down out of the cold north in the second century A.D. Between 250 and 270, Rome fought the Goths in a series of wars that cost the lives of hundreds of thousands on both sides. At length, Rome prevailed, subdued the Goths, and entered into a treaty of peace with them. The peace endured for almost a hundred years.

During that hundred years Rome was badly weakened by internal strife, and by costly military campaigns in Gaul and Persia. The empire itself had been divided into an eastern and a western segment; in 364 A.D. Valentinian I was named Emperor of the West, and his brother Valens, Emperor of the

East. It was this Eastern Roman Empire that was to endure
for a thousand years after the barbarians had taken Rome and
crushed the Western Empire.

About 370, troublesome barbarians called the Huns began
to stir and migrate from their home in eastern Europe. As they
moved west through what is now Russia, they drove other,
weaker peoples before them. Among these peoples were the
Goths, who had been allies of Rome for a century. Forced by
the Huns to flee, the Goths, who by this time were partly
Christian and no longer very barbaric, asked permission to
cross the Danube and move westward into Roman territory.
Eunapius, a historian of that time, has described the scene:

"The multitude of the Scythians [Goths] who escaped from
the murderous savagery of the Huns amounted to not less than
200,000 men of fighting age. These standing upon the river
bank in a state of great excitement, stretched out their hands
from afar with loud lamentations, and earnestly supplicated
that they might be allowed to cross over the river, bewailing
the calamity that had befallen them, and promising that they
would faithfully adhere to the Imperial alliance if this boon
were granted them."

Valens, the Emperor of the East, regarded the Goths as
weaklings and cowards. Although it was risky to let so many
barbarians cross into his territory, Valens decided to admit
them, on condition that they surrender their weapons and
swear loyalty to him as emperor. And so a huge body of Goths
passed peacefully onto Roman soil with the emperor's blessing.

But the Roman officials who were placed in charge of these
Goths were corrupt. They began to exploit and mistreat the
refugees. The Goths took advantage of the corruptness of the
Roman officials to build up a store of weapons. They quietly
vowed to avenge themselves for the outrages the Romans were
committing on their wives and children.

Meanwhile a second wave of Gothic refugees came fleeing

westward. Valens, worried now about the unrest in the area—
now Turkey and Bulgaria—refused to let these new Goths
across the border. But they slipped over anyway, by rafts, and
allied themselves to the Goths already within the Roman
borders.

Discontent and tension were creating an explosive situation.
The Romans, by a clumsy attempt to restore order, succeeded
only in touching off a rebellion.

It happened when the Roman officials, Lupicinus and Maximus, invited the Gothic chieftains Fritigern and Alavivus to
a banquet. Lupicinus secretly planned to fill the Goths with
wine and have them murdered. Midway through the feast, the
Romans fell on the Gothic bodyguard. Fritigern and Alavivus,
hearing the uproar, rushed from the table and drew their
swords. In the battle that followed, Alavivus was cut down,
but Fritigern escaped, determined now to seek revenge on the
Romans for this treachery. "In this way," a Gothic historian
wrote some centuries later, "these valiant men gained the
chance they had longed for—to be free to die in battle rather
than to perish of hunger—and immediately took arms to kill
the generals Lupicinus and Maximus."

Even now, Lupicinus underestimated the Goths. He took
the field against them and was killed. The arms of the Roman
troops fell into possession of the Goths.

A fierce uprising of the Goths followed. With all their old
savagery, the barbarians raged through the Roman district
of Thrace. The historian Ammianus Marcellinus writes that
"without distinction of age or sex all places were ablaze with
slaughter and great fires, sucklings were torn from the very
breasts of their mothers and slain, matrons and widows whose
husbands had been killed before their eyes were carried off,
boys of tender or adult age were dragged away over the dead
bodies of their parents."

Emperor Valens had been busy waging war against Persia,

but now he rushed back to Constantinople to deal with the Gothic uprising in Thrace. Marshaling his troops, he sent also for help from his young nephew Gratian, the Emperor of the West at Rome.

The conflict that followed was of a sort with which history has abounded. The Romans, who had been fighting wars successfully for hundreds of years, had very strong ideas about how it should be done. They believed in highly organized infantry formations, armed with spear and sword. The Goths did not have the benefit of iron discipline and great generals. They invented their tactics as they went along, and fought in informal units. The Romans were puzzled by this kind of guerilla warfare. They did not understand an enemy that refused to form a visible pattern of battle, but struck at random. In their earlier days, the Romans had been able to adapt their battle array to fit the circumstances, as we saw at the battle of Zama. But now they had been supreme too long. They were set in their ways. They had lost the flexibility of strategy which is the essence of attaining victory.

The Goths numbered many hundreds of thousands. Nor were they mere wild men; many had served in Roman armies, and knew how to wield sword, pike, and battle-ax with skill. They fought out of *laagers*, or wagon-forts. Arranging a group of wagons in a circle, they would dart out to give battle, then quickly return to their wall of wagons when trouble appeared. Thus they had what amounted to movable fortresses that could protect them no matter where they fought.

Under the generals Trajan and Profuturus, Valens' legions met with early success against the rebellious Goths. But at a place called Salices, in what is now Bulgaria, the Goths held firm. They settled down behind the rampart of their wagons and stayed there for seven days. The Romans hoped to starve them out, but then news came that thousands of additional Goths were crossing the Danube and invading Thrace. The siege had to be lifted as the Roman legions went to the defense of the beleaguered towns.

As 378 opened, the situation looked grave for Rome, and Valens must have cursed the day he ever let the Goths cross into his territory. The Empire of the East was infested with barbarians, now, and more were arriving daily.

Valens appointed a new commander-in-chief, Sebastianus. This general selected a corps of 2,000 picked men, and made his headquarters at the important city of Adrianople, 137 miles northwest of Constantinople, the Eastern Empire's capital. From there, Sebastianus struck at night, driving the Goths under Fritigern back. Fritigern had been attempting without success to capture Adrianople. Now he fell back to the open country, where the Romans could not defeat him.

Sebastianus realized that a formal army of Roman regiments could not accomplish anything against the Goths. Guerrilla warfare could be coped with only by small, highly trained bands of guerillas. Valens disagreed. The emperor, hearing of Sebastianus' early success against Fritigern, immediately set out for Adrianople at the head of a large army.

Fritigern sent out peace feelers. Valens mocked the envoys. Establishing a camp just outside the walls of Adrianople, the emperor and his army set out for the Gothic encampment, eight miles away.

The Goths were cooped up in one of their impregnable wagon-forts, or laagers. Fritigern was in a secure position, difficult to attack. But his forces were not at full strength, and he was worried. His cavalry, under the chieftains Alatheus and Saphrax, was away gathering supplies. But for their absence, Fritigern might have attacked at that moment. It was a blisteringly hot day—August 9, 378—and the Romans were tired after their sweaty march from Adrianople. Valens' cavalry surrounded the Gothic laager, while the footsore infantry lagged behind.

Unable to attack with his own cavalry away, Fritigern stalled for time. He sent an ambassador out to Valens to ask for peace—strictly as a delaying ruse.

Valens, though, was perfectly willing to stall also, so that his troops, both hungry and thirsty, would have time to rest. He went along with the ruse and pretended to be interested in negotiating peace. To gain time, though, Valens insisted that the ambassadors Fritigern had sent were of too lowly a rank.

"Send me nobles," Valens said loftily, "and I will negotiate with them."

Fritigern was delighted to find the emperor countering his delaying tactics with stalling maneuvers of his own. While the hocus-pocus of exchanging peace terms was going on, the Gothic cavalry under Alatheus and Saphrax was returning— along with a battalion of men from a related tribe, the Alans.

A corps of archers that had accompanied the Roman ambassador foolishly panicked and opened fire on the Gothic laager. These men were not Romans, but Iberians from Spain, poorly trained. It seemed to the returning Gothic cavalry that the laager was under attack. Alatheus and Saphrax immediately went to the defense, while the Alans descended from the hills "like a thunderbolt," as Ammianus Marcellinus writes.

The Gothic cavalry rode boldly into the Roman cavalry line. The Goths scattered the surprised Roman right wing and turned to the Roman left wing. Within moments all the Roman horsemen had been driven into retreat, leaving the weary infantry exposed.

Fritigern chose this moment to burst from the laager with his own infantry. Let Ammianus Marcellinus describe the confusion of the hapless Roman legions:

"The different companies became so huddled together that hardly anyone could pull out his sword, or draw back his arm, and because of clouds of dust the heavens could no longer be seen, and echoed with frightful cries. Hence the arrows whirling death from every side always found their mark with fatal effect, since they could not be seen beforehand nor guarded against."

The Romans were hemmed in, packed together too tightly to create a battle formation. The slaughter was frightful as the Gothic infantry marched in, while the barbarian cavalry kept the Romans from fleeing. Ammianus tells us, "Then you might see the barbarian towering in his fierceness, hissing or shouting, fall with legs pierced through, or his right hand cut off, sword and all, or his side transfixed, and still, in the last gasp of life, casting round him defiant glances." The plain ran red with blood, much of it Roman blood. Men slipped in the bloody stream and were killed by their own weapons. Bodies were heaped high.

Valens drew back as the extent of the rout became evident. Sometime toward evening, he perished. How he died is uncertain. Some say that he was overwhelmed by the Goths on the battlefield, others that he withdrew to a nearby cottage, suffering from an arrow wound, and was there found and killed by a Gothic searching party. At any rate, the emperor died that day, along with the generals Trajan and Sebastianus, many nobles, and 40,000 Roman soldiers.

The defeat rocked the world. The Romans had lost battles before, but never so decisively. Never had barbarians made Roman legionaries look so utterly incompetent at the art of war. From first to last the Romans had been outguessed and baffled by the Goths.

So far as purely military history goes, the significance of the battle of Adrianople lies in the fact that it ended forever the supremacy of the Roman infantry. As one writer puts it, "That evening the sun set for all time on the glory of the legions, the infantry who had been the foundation of Roman world power, and a thousand years' era of cavalry supremacy was ushered in." The Romans heretofore had used cavalry more for decorative purposes than anything else. The real backbone of the army had been the foot soldiers. But the savage charge of the Gothic cavalry had taught the Romans that the old order of military strategy was changing, and they had best adapt to the new situation. When Valens' successor, Theodosius, rebuilt the Roman army, he gave the cavalry the burden of responsibility, and within a century the infantry, once predominant, no longer played a major role in Roman warfare.

The downfall of the infantry was one result of Adrianople. There was a political result, too, of far greater importance to history. The battle left Rome at the mercy of the Goths, but there was still strength in the old empire, and Fritigern failed to capture the city of Adrianople. Instead, he moved off to plunder Thrace.

The new emperor, Theodosius, conceived a plan for pacifying the Goths that was as damaging as Valens' original decision to let them cross the Danube. Theodosius invited the Goths to become soldiers of Rome. He would grant them the right to occupy Thrace, he said, if they would swear loyalty and become Roman soldiers.

Peace was thus restored—but at a tremendous cost. An army of Romans was transformed into an army of Goths fighting for the Roman emperor. As the fourth century ended, the Goths had complete control of the Roman army. They had conquered it bloodlessly, by joining it, after smashing it violently at Adrianople. The direct result of the Roman defeat at Adrianople was the recruiting of Gothic soldiers for the new Roman army, and for the first time in Roman history the Roman army was not composed of Romans.

It is for this reason that I date the fall of Rome from the battle of Adrianople. So long as there was an army of Romans, Rome might have survived with its old majesty; but once the Romans let the Goths fight their wars for them, the power of the emperor died, and Rome was left at the mercy of the barbarians. A dozen marauding peoples took possession of Roman territory in western Europe, and the new Roman army did little to fend off these barbaric cousins. Soon the Empire of the East was cut off completely from the Empire of the West, with barbarians holding the lands between.

The Eastern Empire clung to independence for ten more centuries. But the Western was gradually nibbled away from without and within. Gothic generals of the Roman army made and unmade Roman emperors. The Gothic prince Alaric dictated terms to Rome for many years, and finally, on August 24, 410, entered the city and burned it. The somber words of the historian Orosius tell of the sad depths to which the city of Augustus had descended:

"Adest Alaricus, trepidam Romam obsidet, turbat, irrumpit." ("Alaric appeared before trembling Rome, laid siege, spread confusion and broke into the city.")

There was the pretense of a Western Empire, whose emperors were named by the Goths, until 476. Then even the pretense was extinguished. Other barbarians invaded Rome, and in 476 the Hun, Odoacer, was proclaimed King of Italy. The Western Empire was dead. The Eastern Empire still had a great many centuries of life, but it had little link save in name to the Roman past.

So, then, some may say Rome fell in 1453, when the Eastern Empire collapsed. Some may say Rome fell in 476, with the triumph of Odoacer.

But the fall of Rome, I believe, can be dated sharply to August 9, 378, when the Goths under Fritigern smashed the Roman legions at Adrianople. As a result of that battle, certain actions were taken which became irreversible, and night rushed down on the empire of the Caesars.

CHAPTER

FIVE

THE BATTLE OF TOURS

Charles Martel

Hurls Back the Arabs

THE Roman Empire had moved to Constantinople, and there endured. In the west, barbarians ruled, and gradually grew less barbaric as the passing of the centuries brought softening ways. The nomads of 250 A.D. became the settled city dwellers of 700 A.D., the heirs of Rome. Though these centuries are often referred to as "the Dark Ages," they were no such thing. They were a time when the civilization of Rome was passing to new, rougher hands, and present-day Europe was being born.

While the barbarians of western Europe were acquiring civilization, though, a new threat to world peace was arising out of Arabia. The Prophet Mohammed had come to power about 630, preaching a warlike religion of conquest, and

Islam-enflamed Arab soldiers had roared like the whirlwind over the east. By 632, at Mohammed's death, Islam ruled only in Arabia, but its successors carried their banners first to Persia, then to Syria, Egypt, and North Africa. The overseas provinces of the Roman Empire of the east, the Byzantine Empire, fell into Moslem hands by 709.

The sons of Islam now turned toward Europe, and began a campaign of conquest that was to last nearly a thousand years. In 711, Spain fell to the Arabs, while other Moslem armies laid siege to Constantinople at Europe's opposite end. Constantinople's time had not yet come; it withstood the siege, and continued to fight off the Moslems for another 700 years. In the west, the Arabs were more successful. They swept through Spain, then ruled by Gothic dukes, and began to move northward across the Pyrenees to make themselves masters of all western Europe.

The breakdown of Roman rule had seen new leaders arise in that part of Europe. A people called the Franks had become dominant in what now is France. The Franks had driven the Huns and Goths from Gaul, under the great King Clovis. By the seventh century, though, the Frankish kings had lost all power. A host of minor princelings ruled small segments of the Frankish kingdom. The descendants of Clovis had become figureheads, and their power had passed to palace officials known as mayors of the palace, but even the mayors of the palace could not extend their sway through all the Frankish territories.

Pepin II, mayor of the palace, died in 714. His son Charles attempted to take Pepin's place, but was blocked by his stepmother, who favored one of her own children by Pepin. Charles was imprisoned in 714, and several years of civil war followed. During the civil uprising Charles escaped from prison and led his followers against the insurgents. Province by province, Charles made himself master of Pepin's old lands—first the province of Austrasia, then Neustria, then Aquitania. By 717 Charles held the title of mayor of the palace, and he appointed a puppet king, Clotaire IV, to occupy the throne of Austrasia.

While this struggle was going on, the lesser dukes of the Frankish provinces were rebelling against the mayor of the palace's authority. Eudo, Duke of Aquitania, was the strongest of these rebel dukes.

This situation of confusion and strife among the Christian rulers of Gaul was made to order for the Arab plan of European conquest. They intended to sweep eastward across all of Europe, cutting Constantinople off from both sides. By 720, the Arabs were across the Pyrenees and into what is now France. They captured Narbonne, held by the Goths, and prepared to move north.

Duke Eudo moved against them and defeated them in 721, at Toulouse. This setback stopped the Islamic tide for a brief while, but by 725 they renewed the attack and made sharp inroads into Gaul, capturing such important cities as Carcassone and Nîmes, and raiding as far north as Burgundy. Dissension on the Arab side prevented the Moslems from taking full advantage of their victories, however.

Moslem dissension ended in 729 when a new general, Abd-ar-Rahman, took command of the attack against Europe. Under his command the Arabs plunged deep into Gaul, heading first for the city of Bordeaux. Duke Eudo met them there, but was soundly defeated. The Arabs took Bordeaux, burned and plundered it, and moved on northward. Abd-ar-Rahman split his forces in two, laying siege to Poitiers with one force, directing the other toward Tours, 60 miles northward.

With the Arabs overrunning his territory, Duke Eudo was compelled to turn to his old enemy Charles, the mayor of the palace. Charles had been fighting in the east, and his valor in warfare had won him the name of Charles Martel—"Charles the Hammer."

In 731 Eudo hurried to Paris and swore allegiance to Charles, ending their enmity of some 15 years. Then Charles moved southward, at the head of his army of Franks, to go to Eudo's defense and drive the Moors from Gaul.

The Arab invaders had completed their conquest of Poitiers by this time, and were continuing the siege of the rich city of Tours, when Charles Martel and his army approached them. It was October 732, just a century after Mohammed's death. Charles Martel was forty-four, and at the height of his strength.

Martel's army was not much more than a rabble. Charles had no riches to pay his soldiers, so they paid themselves with plunder as they fought. When food and booty became scarce, the armies simply broke up. His troops were poorly armed, with only the nobles having horses. They fought with swords, daggers, javelins and axes.

Abd-ar-Rahman's troops, on the other hand, consisted largely of cavalry. They wore little armor, and depended on their speed to protect them, unlike the heavily armored Frankish infantry. The lance and the sword were the chief weapons; bows and arrows were seldom employed.

Although his troops were poorly armed and poorly trained, Charles Martel himself had a keen grasp of strategy. As he marched toward the Arab force, he wrote to Eudo, "If you follow my advice you will not interrupt their march nor precipitate your attack. They are like a torrent, which it is dangerous to stem in its career. . . . Be patient till they have loaded themselves with the encumbrance of wealth. The possession of wealth will divide their counsels and assure your victory."

The advice was shrewd. The Arabs were so heavily loaded

with booty that they could hardly move. Hurriedly, Abd-ar-Rahman ordered the plunder shipped southward, so that his soldiers could fight without worrying about their treasure.

For seven days the two armies faced each other without beginning hostilities. During this week the Moslems relieved themselves of their burdensome treasures while the Franks assembled their forces. Gradually the Moslems fell back toward the south while trying to devise a strategy.

The Moslems knew nothing about fighting a defensive battle. For a hundred years they had been on the offensive, constantly bringing the attack to the enemy. A lightly armored army of horsemen is better suited for attack than defense; foot soldiers can stand firm behind their shields and wait, while cavalry can only charge.

Seeing this, the Moslems resolved to carry the attack themselves. On the eighth day Abd-ar-Rahman gave the order to charge. The thunder of thousands of hooves shook the earth as the unstoppable Arab horsemen plunged wildly toward the Frankish lines.

Charles Martel had drawn his men up in a solid wall. His own battle-hardened troops were at the core of the phalanx. Soldiers of many nations formed the outer lines. It was an international army of Europe, standing against the Arab charge.

And it stood firm. One chronicler's account tells us, "The men of the north stood as motionless as a wall. They were like an impenetrable zone of ice frozen together, and not to be dissolved, as they slew the Arab with the sword."

The accounts of the battle that we have are vague ones. They were written by Christian monks and by Arab historians, and neither side took an impartial view of the conflict. And so we do not know how many men fought in this historic battle, nor how many fell, or even how the stages of the battle unfolded. The accounts are too unreliable to follow.

One monk claims that the Arabs lost 375,000 men that day, the Christians only 1,007. But an Arab chronicler insists that the entire Arab army numbered only 80,000, against a vastly greater number of Franks. We do not know where the truth lies, though it is probably in between.

We do know that Charles Martel carried the day. Charles the Hammer smashed the Arab cavalry ruthlessly, and Abd-ar-Rahman was killed in battle. According to the Christian account of the struggle, when night fell both armies drew back, and in the morning, when the Franks advanced to do battle once again, the Arabs had fled and their tents were empty, with the bulk of their plunder left behind.

The Arab chronicler differs slightly. He maintains that the battle continued into a second day, though the first had been so disastrous for the Arabs:

"The Moslem horsemen dashed fierce and frequent forward against the battalions of the Franks, who resisted manfully, until the going down of the sun. Night parted the two armies; but in the gray of the morning the Moslems returned to the battle.

"Their cavaliers had soon hewn their way into the center of the Christian host. But many of the Moslems were fearful for the safety of the spoil which they had stored in their tents, and a false cry arose in their ranks that some of the enemy were plundering the camp. Whereupon several squadrons of the Moslem horsemen rode off to protect their tents. But it seemed as if they fled, and all the host was troubled.

"And while Abd-ar-Rahman strove to check their tumult, and to lead them back to battle, the warriors of the Franks came around him, and he was pierced through with many spears, so that he died. Then all the host fled before the enemy, and many died in the flight. This deadly defeat of the Moslems, and the loss of the great leader and good cavalier,

Abd-ar-Rahman, took place in the 115th year of the Moslem era [732 A.D.]"

Whatever the actual details of the battle may have been, of the outcome there is no doubt. It was a "deadly defeat" for the Moslems. Their greatest general was slain and their headlong plunge into western Europe was checked by the military genius of Charles Martel.

The battle was a decisive one because it marked the last time the Arabs would attempt to invade Europe from the west. Charles Martel had choked off their advance at a critical time in world history. Had he fallen on the field at Tours, instead of Abd-ar-Rahman, there would have been no holding back the Moors, and they would have made all Europe their own. Perhaps today the nations we know as France, Germany, and England would all be Mohammedan countries, except for the valor of Charles Martel.

As it was, the Arabs were compelled to retreat in confusion, and then were forced to devote their attention to a series of revolts in North Africa. During this time, they were unable to renew their attacks on Europe. They maintained a foothold in Spain for many centuries, but never again succeeded in crossing the Pyrenees.

What Charles Martel had won for Europe was time: time to acquire a greater understanding of the nature of power; time to realize that a thousand quarreling dukes could not withstand an invader a thousandth as well as one strong king ruling a unified land. In the nine years of his life after the battle of Tours, Charles Martel concentrated on forging that unified land. He drove the Arabs out of southern Gaul, he added Eudo's lands to his kingdom after that duke's death, and he subdued the wild tribes of Germany and set the stage for the inclusion of the Germanic lands into the Frankish kingdom.

All this time Charles Martel's title was simply mayor of the palace. But his son Pepin the Short, who succeeded him in 741, was ten years later named king of the Franks, replacing the figurehead King Childeric III.

It was Pepin's son, and the grandson of Charles Martel, who completed the task of welding the scattered states of Europe into one vast empire of Christianity, a new empire of the west that succeeded the long dead Roman Empire. Without Charles Martel's victory at Tours, his grandson could never have achieved that great accomplishment, of founding a Holy Roman Empire that one historian has called "the central event of the Middle Ages."

History knows that grandson of Charles Martel well. He also bore the name of Charles. Charles the Great, he was called—the Emperor Charlemagne.

THE BATTLE OF HASTINGS

William Conquers England

IN Caesar's time Rome had occupied an island at Europe's western shore, but the Romans had long since abandoned Britain to its own barbaric people. The island held a strangely magnetic appeal for conquerors, though. Wave after wave of invaders swept across the sea to Britain.

The invaders came, conquered, and were absorbed. First the Celts invaded and then Germanic tribes like the Angles, the Saxons, and the Jutes migrated westward and settled in Britain, and soon came to think of the island as their own. The original inhabitants and the Celts were driven into the mountain fastnesses on the western side of the island. The island became known as England—"Angle-Land."

Kings reigned all over England. Five separate kingdoms bickered on the small island until 827, when Egbert, King of Wessex, made himself supreme in all the Anglo-Saxon kingdoms. His grandson, King Alfred, brought glory to the island.

New invaders from Scandinavia threatened England. The old invaders, now the settled inhabitants, resisted. Danes obtained a foothold and made permanent settlements in England, but under King Alfred the power of the Danes was limited to eastern England alone. For a century, Dane fought Anglo-Saxon in England, and for a time the Danish King Canute was also King of England.

England absorbed these invaders and made them their own, as it had hundreds of years earlier absorbed the Celts, the Angles, the Saxons and the Jutes. By 1042, an Anglo-Saxon king again ruled in England, recognized by Danes and Anglo-Saxons alike.

This new king's name was Edward the Confessor. In his ancestry many strains of blood were mingled. He was a descendant of King Alfred, and was the son of the last Anglo-Saxon king before Canute, Ethelred the Unready. But Edward's mother came from across the waters in France. She was the daughter of Richard, Duke of Normandy.

In those years France was not yet a nation. Charlemagne's empire had been divided, and France had again fallen into a confusion of many states and many rulers. The dukes of Normandy were among the most powerful of those rulers. They were descendants of Norsemen who had come to settle in northern France about 900. Just as Danes had become absorbed into England, the Norsemen had become French. French was the language they spoke, and French were their customs.

Edward, then, was half Anglo-Saxon, half Norman. He was raised in Normandy, and had lived there from earliest childhood until his recall to the English throne in 1042. When he returned to England, he brought with him Norman friends and advisers, Norman ways. They contrasted sharply with the rougher, cruder ways of the Anglo-Saxons.

Edward was childless. As his life drew near to a close, all

England wondered who would succeed him on the throne. There were many claimants. Magnus II, the King of Norway, insisted that he had a right to the throne, as a successor to the Danish King Hardecanute, whom Edward had succeeded in England. Godwin of Wessex, an Anglo-Saxon noble, claimed the throne by virtue of his descent from King Alfred. And from across the English Channel came the claim of Edward's cousin, William, Duke of Normandy.

No one took the claim of King Magnus of Norway very seriously in England. But the country was divided between the rival claims of Godwin and William. Which would it be? Who would succeed Edward?

Edward's Norman advisers had succeeded in getting Godwin banished from England in 1051. He and his sons took flight and it seemed that the Normans would be supreme in England. Duke William crossed the Channel to visit his royal cousin Edward and, many believe, Edward told William at this meeting, "You will be King of England when I die."

No matter what promise King Edward may or may not have made to Duke William, the sympathies of the English people were still with Godwin. Poor Edward, half English, half French, bowed to public demand and allowed Godwin to return to England and resume his noble rank.

Godwin died in 1053, and his son Harold II succeeded him as Earl of Wessex and as chief claimant to the English throne. Harold was popular among the English. King Edward recognized this, and gave Harold great responsibilities. During the last years of the old king's life, Edward and Harold virtually shared the throne. Edward still privately favored his Norman cousin. But the English people wanted Harold.

In 1065, Harold visited Duke William at the Norman court. Just how he got there, and why, is a matter of some doubt. One chronicler tells us that Edward, "who loved William as a brother or a son," felt "the hour of his death approaching"

and, in order to leave no doubt that the Norman would succeed him, "dispatched Harold to William in order that he
might confirm his promise by an oath." On route, Harold was
shipwrecked and fell into the hands of another French nobleman. William rescued Harold from this other count, and
Harold, of his own accord, swore allegiance to William and
promised that he would support the Norman duke as heir to
the English throne.

The other version of the story is much stranger. According
to this version, Harold agreed to visit William at King Edward's request, but did not intend to swear an oath of loyalty.
The crafty Duke William, though, persuaded Harold to swear
such an oath. Harold agreed, not intending to keep the oath.
Here is how Sir Edward Creasy tells the story of what happened:

"Before a full assembly of the Norman barons, Harold was
required to do homage to Duke William, as the heir-apparent
of the English crown. Kneeling down, Harold placed his hands
between those of the duke, and repeated the solemn form, by
which he acknowledged the duke as his lord, and promised to
him fealty and true service.

"But William exacted more. He had caused all the bones
and relics of saints, that were preserved in the Norman monas-
teries and churches, to be collected into a chest, which was
placed in the council room, covered over with a cloth of gold.
On the chest of relics, which were thus concealed, was laid
a missal.

"The duke then solemnly addressed his titular guest and
real captive, and said to him, 'Harold, I require thee, before
this noble assembly, to confirm by oath the promises which
thou hast made me, to assist me in obtaining the crown of
England after King Edward's death, to marry my daughter
Adela, and to send me thy sister, that I may give her in
marriage to one of my barons.'

"Harold, once more taken by surprise, and not able to deny his former words, approached the missal, and laid his hand on it, not knowing that the chest of relics was beneath. The old Norman chronicler, who describes the scene most minutely, says, when Harold placed his hand on it, the hand trembled, and the flesh quivered; but he swore, and promised upon his oath, to take Ele [Adela] to wife, and to deliver up England to the duke, and thereunto to do all in his power, according to his might and wit, after the death of Edward, if he himself should live . . . so help him God.

"Many cried, 'God grant it!' and when Harold rose from his knees, the duke made him stand close to the chest, and took off the pall that had covered it, and showed Harold upon what holy relics he had sworn; and Harold was sorely alarmed at the sight."

Whether by trickery or of his own free will, Harold definitely swore an oath in 1065 to give William the throne. The gentle King Edward died on January 5, 1066, and all England clamored for the well-liked Harold to mount the throne. Word was given out by the English nobles that Edward, on his deathbed, had named Harold as his successor. Actually Edward had probably done no such thing, since he almost certainly favored the claim of his cousin William. But if William became king, England would be ruled by a foreigner, a Norman. The Anglo-Saxon nobles much preferred Harold, who was of their own blood.

Harold had sworn an oath to William. He now chose to disregard it. On January 7, 1066, he was anointed King of England, and received the golden crown, the scepter, and the battle-ax that were the symbols of his authority.

William of Normandy raged. By messenger he angrily reminded Harold of the solemn oath he had sworn.

Harold replied, "It is true that I took an oath, but it was forced on me. And I promised what was not mine. The will of the country calls me to the throne. That will is stronger than any oath I swore to you. I must obey it."

Hearing this, William revealed the story of the oath to the other rulers of Europe, and attracted wide sympathy. Even the Pope approved when William declared he would go to war to win the throne of England.

Harold was in a hard-pressed position. Several of the northern earls of England refused to recognize him as king for a full three months after his coronation; William was making threatening gestures in Normandy; and Harold Haardraade, son of King Magnus and now King of Norway himself, had revived Magnus' old claim to England's throne, adding to Harold's woes.

Harold's army was not a strong one. It consisted of two forces—the fyrd, a national militia recruited in emergencies, and the housecarls, a smaller body of paid professional soldiers. The fyrd was largely made up of farmers who had to be drafted in times of war, and like all draftees, these men had little interest in killing or being killed.

William, on the other hand, was a warlike man who ruled over a warlike race. One writer of the time said of the Normans, "They can hardly live without war, fierce in rushing against the enemy, and when strength fails of success, ready to use strategem." Besides his well-disciplined men, William was able to call on the best soldiers of Europe, men from such kingdoms as Burgundy, Aquitaine, Flanders, Poitou and even from Italy. Since the Pope backed William, it became almost an act of Christian duty to join the campaign against Harold. And William promised to make all his soldiers noblemen in England after the conquest, a powerful lure.

Through the spring and summer of 1066, preparations for war continued on both sides of the English Channel. Harold had no way of knowing when the invasion was coming, and could not keep the fyrd soldiers away from their farms indefinitely. Harold waited until September 8, and then decided no invasion was coming. He disbanded the fyrd and dispersed his fleet.

Hardly had the hapless king sent his army home than stunning news came: "England is invaded!"

But not by William. King Harold Haardraade of Norway had unexpectedly landed in the north. With 200 warships, 300 other vessels, and the best fighting men of Norway, he had come to assert his claim to England's throne.

Harold turned to meet this new threat. Hastily he reassembled his scattered army and marched north. This left the southern coast open to invasion from Normandy, but there was no help for it; Harold could deal with only one enemy at a time, and Harold Haardraade was already here.

The Norwegian king was marching through Yorkshire, burning and looting as he went. On September 20, he took the city of York, decimated the armies of the northern earls Edwin and Morcar, and was preparing for further attack when King Harold unexpectedly overtook him. A furious march had brought Harold to York in only four days.

The Battle of Stamford Bridge, on September 25, saw the death of Harold Haardraade and the end of the Norwegian threat to England. Harold and his soldiers fought bravely and well, destroying the flower of the Norwegian nobility, and leaving the field so strewn with bodies that a chronicler two generations later wrote that great heaps of bones still could be seen on the battlefield.

It was a wonderful victory for Harold, but a terribly costly one. The Norwegians had exacted a high price for defeat. Many of Harold's finest soldiers had fallen at Stamford Bridge. The army of England was badly weakened by the fray.

William, meanwhile, unaware of Harold Haardraade's invasion plans, was still assembling his own army. By the middle of August he was ready. The chronicler William of Jumièges claims that his army numbered 50,000 knights and 10,000 commoners, and that William's navy counted 3,000 ships. Modern historians regard this as an impossibly large number, and feel that the true size of William's force was perhaps a tenth as great.

For a full month William's army remained in port while a strong northeast gale blew. The soldiers grew impatient, but William used the time well, training his men to a peak of perfection. On September 12, the wind became westerly, and the Normans were able to put to sea. They sailed to a different port, from which the Channel crossing would be easier. Again the winds grew fierce, and many of William's ships were wrecked. The troops were restless. It seemed that even the elements were against them.

They were wrong. William could not have had better luck than to be cooped up in port for so many weeks. Had he sailed for England on August 12, as originally planned, he would have had to meet Harold's army at its full strength. As it was, unfavorable winds penned William just long enough to allow Harold Haardraade to invade England. The English army that William ultimately faced was weary and weak after its earlier struggle against the Norwegians.

What would history be like had William invaded in August? Would Harold have defeated him, only to fall to Harold Haardraade? Would England have become a Norwegian possession? Or would Harold have prevailed in both encounters, and maintained the Anglo-Saxon rule in England? Ah, those are questions for the seers to answer. Mortals can only guess.

The wind finally relented on September 27, and the Normans set sail at midnight. William led the way in his flagship *Mora*, a great lantern lashed to her mast to show the way for the fleet. The small Norman boats, each bearing 30 or 40 soldiers, navigated the Channel safely, and landed at Pevensey

Bay, in Sussex, on the 29th of September, 1066. It was the last time conquerors would ever set foot on English soil.

These conquerors set foot uncertainly. As Duke William stepped ashore, he slipped and fell headlong. A great cry of distress went up from the Normans. An evil omen! The duke had fallen while disembarking! But the clever William came to his feet clutching two handfuls of earth, and smiled, and bellowed, "This is no evil omen! This is a sign from God! See, my lords, by the splendor of God, I have taken possession of England with both my hands. It is now mine, and what is mine is yours!"

The Normans were cheered. They swarmed ashore eagerly, taking possession of the beach as though they already owned all of England.

Harold was still at York, celebrating his victory over Harold Haardraade and resting his men, when news reached him, on October 1, that William at last had landed.

Was there to be no end to these invasions? The tired Harold sent word that the fyrd must once again assemble, and that all must march in haste to defend southern England before London was captured, and with it the kingdom.

London is 200 miles south of York. Harold set out on October 2, and reached his capital four days later. He spent the next few days collecting and assembling his forces. William, for his part, had drawn his camp at Hastings, 62 miles southeast of London, gathering his strength before moving north.

Harold might have done well to wait in London until a full army had been collected. But Harold was an impatient, impulsive man, and he was full of pride after his victory over the Norwegians. He resolved to repeat the tactic that had defeated Harold Haardraade: he would march at once to the camp of the enemy, take them by surprise, and overwhelm them. On October 11, he set out for Hastings, while dispatching a fleet of some 70 ships to cut off the Normans' path of retreat to France.

The miracle that Harold's full army had worked at Stamford Bridge was not so easily repeated by a tired, thinned army at Hastings. Harold now had only some 4,000 men at his command, and many of his veteran soldiers had fallen at Stamford Bridge. On October 13, at night, Harold reached Hastings, and camped seven miles north of William's lines.

Harold's brothers Gurth and Leofwine were uneasy about the king's strategy. They saw Harold's tired army, which had fought a bloody battle only a few weeks earlier, and then had marched strenuously to reach Hastings, facing a well-rested and much larger Norman army. And they were worried about the oath Harold had sworn. Privately they felt that William had a right to the throne. Harold, they believed, was risking the wrath of God by breaking an oath sworn on the bones of saints.

Harold stood firm. They urged him to hold back, to let William come to him, but he refused. Then they asked him not to take part in the battle himself. Again he refused, telling them that a king must lead his own troops if he is to be a king at all.

Hilly country separated the two armies, and Harold occupied the high ground. It was a point in his favor. There was forest behind him, and a long steep slope in front of him. The forest would give him an area for retreat, while the steep slope would make a Norman cavalry charge difficult. The English fought only on foot; the Normans had a powerful cavalry, but charging uphill would be a problem for them.

Harold packed his soldiers densely, shoulder to shoulder, to form a solid wall of shields along three sides of the hill. The frontmost men, clad in chain mail and wielding stout shields, were chosen for their strength and bravery. The English were armed with spears, javelins, two-edged swords, and heavy, long-handled axes. They did not use archers.

Harold's plan was to move his shield wall forward in unbroken formation, driving the Normans back and cutting them to pieces. But the English never had time to lead the attack. They arrived at Hastings near midnight, when attack was impossible. It was necessary to wait until dawn to attack. Possibly Harold intended to surprise William shortly after sunrise, but it was William who did the surprising. Harold's tired troops may well have overslept, since a chronicler tells us, "William came against him by surprise before his army was drawn up in battle array."

William must have set out in the hours before dawn to cover the six miles from his camp to his battle position. He deployed his troops in three divisions. In the center were his own Normans. On the left were men of Brittany, under their leader, Count Alan. On the right were the men of many kingdoms, under Eustace of Boulogne. In each of the three wings, light-armed foot soldiers were in the front, heavy-armed infantry in the second rank, and cavalry in the rear. The light-armed men had bows and crossbows, the second rank had spears, and the cavalry wielded long-handled swords.

By 9 in the morning, on Saturday, October 14, 1066, William's men were in battle position. Trumpets rang out across the quiet hillside. The dismayed English hurriedly sprang to battle positions. The Norman poet Robert Wace gives this description of the scene:

"The English stood firm in close ranks, and carried themselves right boldly. Each man had his hauberk on, with his sword girt, and his shield at his neck. Great hatchets were also slung at their necks, with which they expected to strike great blows.

"The Normans brought on the three divisions of their army to attack at different places. They set out in three companies, and in three companies did they fight. The first and second had come up, and then advanced the third, which was the greatest; with that came the duke with his own men, and all moved boldly forward.

"As soon as the two armies were in full view of each other, great noise and tumult arose. You might hear the sound of many trumpets and bugles, and of horns; and then you might see men ranging themselves in line, lifting their shields, raising their lances, bending their bows, handling their arrows, ready for assault and defence.

"The English stood steady to their post, the Normans still moved on; and when they drew near, the English were to be seen stirring to and fro; were going and coming; troops ranging themselves in order; some with their color rising, others turning pale; some making ready their arms; others raising their shields; the brave man rousing himself to fight, the coward trembling at the approach of danger."

Then, Wace relates, the minstrel Taillefer approached Duke William. "I beg a boon, sire!" the minstrel cried. "I have long served you, and you owe me for all such service. Today, so please you, you shall repay it. I beseech you, allow me to strike the first blow in the battle!"

The Norman duke smiled. "I grant it," he said.

And the minstrel rode forward, juggling his sword, tossing it high in the air and catching it again, letting the morning sun glint from his blade. Boldly he rode into the English ranks and struck an Englishman dead with his lance. Another Englishman fell to the minstrel's sword. Then the English swarmed about him, and cut him from his horse. The Normans advanced. The battle had been joined.

"Loud and far resounded the bray of the horns, and the shocks of the lances, the mighty strokes of maces, and the quick clashing of swords," Wace declares. The English wall of shields withstood the first Norman thrust. Dozens of Normans fell before English swords. The archers failed to make a dent in that wall of shields, and soon panicked and began to fall back. "The whole army of the duke was in danger of retreat," writes the chronicler William of Poitiers.

This was the signal for Harold's men to take the offensive—and they made their fatal mistake. The right wing of the shield wall broke, and the English came running down the hill in wild pursuit of the fleeing archers. William's heavy cavalry, surrounded by the retreating Norman front lines, was thrown into confusion. For a moment it looked as though the wild counterattack would succeed. The Norman lines were broken. They were in flight. And where was Duke William? Nowhere to be seen!

"The duke is fallen!" the Normans cried. "The duke is dead!" And terror swept through the ranks of the invaders.

The duke had fallen, but the duke was not dead. William had been knocked from his horse in the confusion. He was the rallying point around which the whole army centered, and had he died then it would have meant certain defeat.

Knowing this, William mounted another horse, and threw back his helmet to show his face to his men. At the top of his lungs he boomed out, "Look at me well! I am still alive, and by the grace of God I shall yet prove victor!"

It was the turning point of the battle. The Normans were cheered at the sight of their duke, rallied, and overcame their panic. They began to re-form their lines.

The English counterattackers, who had only a moment before been driving the foe before them, suddenly found themselves in the midst of a well-organized resistance. They were cut off and had come too far down the hill to return. Hundreds of English were swallowed up by the Norman tide.

William now hit upon a new strategy. He had learned, from his earlier charge, that it was impossible to break the English wall of shields. So long as the English stood firm, the Normans had no chance of victory, and would ultimately have to fall back in retreat—but their line of retreat was blockaded by Harold's navy.

The only hope of the Normans was once again to lure the

English into a counterattack that would break their tightly held formation. Once, the Normans had panicked and the English had followed them down the hill. Would the English follow again, if the Normans retreated a second time?

William made a final attempt to break the wall. He pulled back his infantry and sent his mounted knights to the front line, but the English held firm. Still unwilling to risk a feigned retreat, William ordered his archers into action. Aiming directly at the English would not help; the English simply blocked the arrows with their shields.

"Aim into the air," William told them. "Let the arrows fall on them from above."

A rain of arrows fell on the English, striking many of them in the face, blinding some. Legend has it that one of these arrows struck Harold himself, putting out his right eye. The historian Charles H. Gibbs-Smith has recently attacked this story as a later invention. Gibbs-Smith quotes William of Jumièges, the chronicler who wrote in 1070, as saying simply, "Harold himself . . . fell covered with deadly wounds." And the Bayeux tapestry, a pictorial account of the battle completed no later than 1082, does not appear to show Harold being struck in the eye by an arrow, but simply being cut down by a Norman sword. The earliest reference to the arrow-in-the-eye story appears in the account of William of Malmesbury, completed in 1125.

Perhaps the old story is true, perhaps not. Certainly Harold received a mortal wound in the battle. But the English soldiers, unaware that their king was fallen, held their wall unbroken. At length William had to resort to his ruse. He ordered a general retreat.

The Normans fled slowly, scattering in all directions. And the English followed. Wace tells us:

"Thus they were deceived by the pretended flight, and great mischief thereby befell them. For if they had not moved from their position, it is not likely they would have been conquered at all; but like fools they broke their lines and pursued."

The English mocked the fleeing Normans. In Wace's words, they jeered, "Cowards, you came hither in an evil hour, wanting our lands, and seeking to seize our property, fools that ye were to come! Normandy is too far off, and you will not easily reach it. It is of little use to run back. Unless you can cross the sea at a leap, or can drink it dry, your sons and daughters are lost to you."

The Normans only laughed quietly as they retreated. The English insults were in a foreign language, and fell on deaf ears. Soon the English were hopelessly strung out over the plain. Perhaps Harold had already fallen at this time, or possibly he died afterward—but certainly the English had stopped acting as an army and were moving about as individuals under no general orders.

When William decided the English were thoroughly out of formation, he gave the signal, and the Norman retreat halted. William's men hacked their way back up the hill. The English shield wall, weakened already, gave way completely. Twilight was descending. The shield wall held only in the center, and then the last remnant fell under a Norman charge, and the English fled. The Normans pursued them into the forest, and only a handful escaped.

At sundown, William returned to the battlefield. Harold's body was discovered, and William took it back to camp with him, burying it later at the seashore. The last Anglo-Saxon king of England was dead. The Normans had carried the day.

After two days of rest, William left Hastings and marched north to London, while sending other troops throughout all of the south of England. In the next seven weeks he covered 350 miles, meeting little opposition and conquering every town he reached. By December, William came to London, and on Christmas Day he was crowned King of England. During the years that followed he subdued every city and town of the land, and made himself master of the entire country.

The Norman Conquest transformed England. Once more an alien bloodline was joined to that of England, and Norman joined Celt, Dane, Angle, Saxon, and Jute to create the British Empire. The mixture of strong races, perhaps, explains the strength of Great Britain through the centuries that followed. Never again was she to be conquered, and the blood of Duke William flows in the British monarch to this day.

And if it had been different? Had Harold lived through the day, would he have kept his men from falling into William's trap? If the English shield wall had held firm, William almost certainly would have been defeated. If Harold's army was not thinned by the conflict with Harold Haardraade, William might not have won. Those are big ifs—and our world would be greatly different had they been fulfilled. Anglo-Saxon England could never have become the nation that Anglo-Norman England became. The rude strength of the Normans first had to be grafted to the basic Anglo-Saxon stock. From the hybrid race sprang the men of England's golden age, who carried their civilization across the sea to the thirteen colonies of North America.

Hastings was an all-important battle in world history. Here is the verdict of General Fuller:

"For England, Hastings was not only the most decisive battle ever fought on her soil, but also the most decisive in her history, in fact, there is no other battle which compares with it in importance. In the place of a loosely-knit and undisciplined country was substituted a unified and compact kingdom under a firm and hereditary central authority, a king who knew how to combine feudalism with personal government."

THE BATTLE OF ORLÉANS

Joan of Arc Saves France

WHILE Norman kings made England strong in the centuries that followed, France remained disunited. The King of England also ruled Normandy, and so England had a bridgehead in France. Not for many hundreds of years did the English abandon the hope of adding all France to their kingdom.

Foolish King John of England lost most of England's French possessions to King Philip Augustus of France at the beginning of the thirteenth century. But England struck back. In the Hundred Years' War—which actually lasted more than a century, from 1337 to 1453—England sought to master France.

Edward III of England was the son of an English king and the nephew of a French king. Edward also ruled as Duke of Aquitaine in France. In 1339 Edward announced his claim to the throne of France, and launched an invasion. It was 1066 again in reverse.

Twenty years of war brought a brief peace. Edward agreed to renounce the title of King of France in return for 3,000,000 gold crowns, the cities of Calais and Ponthieu, and a greatly enlarged Duchy of Aquitaine. But the treaty was poorly kept, and warfare continued. In 1414 the ambitious young King Henry V of England revived Edward III's old claim to the French throne, and invaded France.

Henry raged through France, recaptured Normandy, and brought the French king to his knees. In 1420, by the Treaty of Troyes, King Charles VI of France agreed to recognize Henry as the heir to his throne. By the terms of the treaty, France and England would be united in one kingdom after Charles' death. Charles' own son, known as the dauphin, was barred from the throne.

But death visited both kings within two years. Henry V died in August 1422, and Charles VI two months later. The heir to the English throne was Henry's nine-month-old son, who in October was proclaimed "Henry VI, by the grace of God, King of France and England."

The disinherited dauphin refused to accept this. Within ten days he had himself proclaimed Charles VII, King of France. Once again, war threatened between England and France. On the one hand, the King of England was a baby; on the other, the self-proclaimed King of France was a boy of nineteen— and a weak and lazy boy at that. Since neither land had a strong king, the burdens of leadership in the struggle would have to fall to others.

In England, that burden fell to John, Duke of Bedford, uncle of the infant Henry VI. In France, however, the lot went to one of history's most remarkable figures—Joan of Arc, the Maid of Orléans.

Joan was born about 1412, daughter of a well-to-do farmer

of Domremy. Her early life was unremarkable, but when she was in her thirteenth year, she began to hear voices, voices that she said came from God. Several times a week, Joan declared, she was visited by saints, usually Saint Catherine and Saint Margaret, sometimes Saint Michael as well. They came to her in a cloud of heavenly light, calling her "Joan the Maid, Daughter of God."

The war between England and France was going poorly for France while Joan was hearing her voices. City after city had fallen to English armies by siege. The English already occupied Normandy. Burgundy, whose duke refused to accept the authority of any king of France, had allied itself with the English invaders. Paris was in English hands. The largest French city still remaining in the possession of the Dauphin Charles, the uncrowned Charles VII, was Orléans, 77 miles southwest of Paris—and Orléans was under siege by the enemy.

An English army of 5,000 men surrounded the city in 1428, under the command of the Earl of Salisbury. Orléans was vital to Charles. The English were already masters of everything to the north; if Orléans fell, they would have no difficulty making the entire kingdom their own.

Orléans, a wealthy city and a populous one, was well able to hold out in a lengthy siege. It boasted strong walls on three of its four sides, with moats to ward off enemy attackers. On the fourth side, the southern, the city opened onto the Loire River, and a bridge led to the suburbs to the south. This bridge was strongly fortified, with towers at each end housing garrisons. Over this bridge, the people of Orléans could communicate with the cities to the south even when besieged.

Lord Salisbury rightly realized that if he took this bridge, he would have the town. On October 23, 1428, his men stormed the bridge and took the southern tower. But the French broke the bridge near the north bank to keep the

English from entering the city. Now Orléans was completely cut off—and since the English held the southern tower, they could menace the city with cannon.

Salisbury himself was killed by a stray splinter of cannon shot while looking out a window of this tower, and command passed on October 27 to the Earl of Suffolk. He continued the siege. Cannon were employed on both sides, making this the first siege in which artillery was used to any real extent, not only to breach walls but to destroy soldiers.

The siege dragged on through November and December. Suffolk had six forts built around the walls of Orléans, and began to dig trenches to connect the forts. But the winter-frozen ground was hard, and supplies were running low. Little was accomplished during the winter. In February 1429, a provision convoy safely reached the besiegers and, thus fortified, they resumed building forts and trenches. Soon English forts surrounded Orléans on all sides.

Within the blockaded city, hunger was now becoming a force to reckon with. A trickle of supplies still was reaching Orléans through the eastern side of the blockade, where the English forces were weakest. Despite this, starvation was taking its toll in the city. The people of Orléans, seeing no end to the siege, offered to surrender—not to the English, but to the Duke of Burgundy. They would give up in return for having their city made neutral.

The English leader, Bedford, would not hear of it. "We can wait," he said. "They'll be starved out soon."

To the south, at Chinon, the Dauphin Charles waited daily to hear of the fall of Orléans. He made plans to escape to Spain or Scotland. Cowardly and uncertain, he was ready to abandon his claim to the throne and run. Only the urging of his advisers and his queen led him to stay.

And at this point, with Orléans about to fall and the dauphin wavering, Joan of Arc's voices spoke clearly to her.

"You must leave your home," they told the seventeen-year-old girl, "and go to the dauphin. You are the chosen instrument of God who will drive the English from Orléans and lead the dauphin to Rheims, where he will be crowned king at the cathedral."

Joan never questioned these voices. She calmly told her parents of her holy mission. "I'd sooner see you drowned than go to the army camp," her father blustered. But Joan prevailed. She persuaded an uncle to take her to Vaucouleurs, where one of the dauphin's generals, Robert de Baudricourt, was in command. There, she explained her mission to the general.

Baudricourt thought she was out of her mind. But she continued to plead with him, and he was won over by her piety, her purity, her sincerity. He offered her a horse and an escort of six soldiers. Still obeying the bidding of her voices, Joan cut her hair, donned the armor of a man, and rode to the dauphin's court at Chinon.

Word of her strange mission got there before her. The dauphin, to test her, arranged to meet her in a hall where 300 people were gathered. Although he deliberately dressed in simple clothes, Joan picked him out at once. Kneeling before him, she declared, "Most noble Dauphin, the King of Heaven announces to you by me that you shall be anointed and crowned king in the city of Rheims."

It seemed like a miracle. Joan's simplicity and earnestness must have glimmered like a beacon among the war-weary, pessimistic courtiers at Chinon. And in those days of religious belief, no one questioned the fact that Joan really did hear voices. The only problem was, were they really voices from God, or was it the Devil playing a prank on the innocent maid?

The dauphin himself was probably too worldly a man to put much faith in the reality of Joan's voices. But he sensed their importance as propaganda. If the people of France learned that God was on their side, speaking through the mouth of a girl, they would fight with redoubled enthusiasm. The dauphin consulted the Church. After all, he did not want to be accused of allying himself to a witch. The bishops studied Joan's claims and gave them their blessing: "She speaks as from God," they agreed.

An army was assembled, some 4000 men, and on April 27, 1429, it set out for Orléans to lift the siege. At its head rode the Maid, in a suit of brilliant white armor flashing blindingly in the sun, and carrying a banner on which was blazoned the words JHESUS MARIA and an image of Christ.

Joan's voices told her that the army should enter Orléans from the north. But this happened to be the point of greatest English strength, and the dauphin's generals, without telling Joan, quietly brought the army in from the south. At first Joan did not realize she had been deceived. But the next morning she saw that Orléans lay to the north.

Angrily she confronted Dunois, a cousin of the dauphin, who came out from the city to meet her. With no respect for his high rank, she harangued him at once. "Was it at your advice that my soldiers came to this side of the river?" she demanded.

"We thought it wisest," Dunois replied.

"The advice of the Lord is more certain and wise than yours," she retorted. "You thought to have deceived me, but you have deceived yourselves; for I bring you the greatest help that has ever been brought to knight or city, seeing that it is the help of the King of Heaven."

Joan ordered that an attack at once be made on Saint Jean le Blanc, the nearest English fort, on the south side of the river. The soldiers with Joan objected; it was more important first to get the provisions convoyed into hungry Orléans. Joan agreed. But a strong wind blew from the northeast, preventing the barges from crossing.

"We will cross," Joan declared. And, as night fell, the wind unexpectedly changed directions. It blew now from the west. Under cover of darkness the provisions and the entire army crossed the Loire. Word passed through the ranks—and reached the now worried English—that Joan had worked another miracle.

During a storm Joan rode into the town by night, from the north, as she had been commanded to do. So far there had been no battle—but Joan was in the city, and Orléans rejoiced. They felt certain that the Maid had divine guidance. On April 29, Joan marched in triumph through Orléans.

The town was still surrounded by the English, though somehow Joan and her convoy of provisions had slipped within. Joan now wrote to Talbot, one of the English commanders, telling him that the Lord ordered the English to go home. Talbot replied insultingly. The next day, Joan went to the bridge, and shouted across to Sir William Glasdale, who led the force of English holding the southern tower, that he should surrender in the name of God. But Glasdale, who like all his comrades thought Joan was a sorceress, roared back foul accusations, and warned Joan, "When we catch you, we will burn you for the witch you are!"

Joan wept with shame and indignation. But the English were cowed by her. Four days later, when reinforcements and more supplies reached Orléans, Joan rode out to meet them, and the English shrank back into their forts and offered no resistance while fresh French troops entered the city under their very noses.

The next day, Joan's soldiers attacked the fort of Saint Loup. They were driven back when soldiers of another English fort, Saint Pouair, came to the aid of Saint Loup. Seeing her troops in flight, Joan spurred her horse and rode into their midst, waving her banner and crying, *"Hari!* Go boldly in among the English! Go boldly in!"

Joan's banner rallied the troops, and Saint Loup fell to the French assault. The garrison was put to the sword, except for a few men spared at Joan's request. The first encounter between the armies had brought victory for France, and Orléans joyfully rang its church bells in tribute to the Maid's leadership.

The next day, May 5, was Ascension Day, and Joan spent it in prayer. On May 6, it was decided to attack the English forts to the south of the city. A breakthrough had to be made, because it was rumored that the Duke of Bedford was marching on Orléans with reinforcements.

"The siege will be lifted in five days," Joan calmly told her men.

She was still eager to avoid bloodshed, and a third time commanded the English to surrender. A third time they refused offensively, and again Joan wept.

On May 6, the attack began. The French crossed the river in boats, and attacked the fort of Saint Jean de Blanc. The English fled to the stronger fort of Augustins, which the French generals thought was impregnable. They began to withdraw, and the English emerged from the fort to give chase.

"Attack!" Joan cried. "Do not retreat!"

The French whirled. Led by Joan, they drove the English out of the Augustins Fort as well as Saint Jean de Blanc. The surviving English took refuge in the Tourelles, the southern tower of the broken bridge across the Loire. Five hundred English archers and men-at-arms occupied this critical fort, but now that the French held the other forts to the south, it was completely cut off.

The French generals argued for a siege. Joan was bolder than they, and ordered an immediate attack. To her confessor, though, she said, "Keep near me throughout the day, for I shall have much to do, more than ever before. Blood will flow from my body above my breast."

The French troops massed at the captured Augustins Fort. Other soldiers bombarded the Tourelles from an island in the Loire, while workmen hurried to repair the bridge so an attack on the tower could be made from north as well as south. At 7 o'clock on the morning on May 7, the trumpets sounded for the attack, and the dull boom of cannon rolled over the Loire.

A deep ditch surrounded the Tourelles, and this had to be scaled by ladders, while the defenders hacked away from above. Joan leaped into the ditch and, planting her banner at its edge, thrust a ladder against the wall. As she began to scale it, an arrow from above sliced through her armor and wounded her severely between the neck and shoulder.

The English sent men down to capture the fallen Maid, but the French rescued her in time. She was taken to the rear of the lines and her armor removed. The arrow was taken out— some say she drew it out with her own hands—and, though she trembled, she quickly regained her strength.

News that Joan was wounded had dampened French spirits. But she told them not to retreat. Pointing to the tower, she cried, "By my God, you shall soon enter in there. Do not doubt it. When you see my banner wave against the wall, to your arms again. The fort is yours. For the present rest a little, and take some food and drink."

Joan prayed, and had her wound dressed, and soon afterward was ready once again to lead the attack. Now she could not carry her banner herself, and a soldier carried it at her side. The English, who had thought she was dead, were appalled to see her return. She forged forward, and her ban-

ner carrier touched the wall of the fort with it. It was the
signal for an all-out offensive. The French placed their ladders
and swarmed up into the tower.

Joan confronted Sir William Gladsdale, who had mocked
her the week before. "Surrender, surrender to the King of
Heaven," she cried out. "Ah, you have foully wronged me
with your words, but I have great pity on your soul and the
souls of your men."

Gladsdale spat and turned away. A moment later, as he
strode onto the drawbridge, a cannon shot from the city
knocked him into the Loire. The Tourelles had fallen. Three
hundred of the English were dead, the rest prisoners. The
bridge repairs were completed, and Joan made a triumphal
entry into the city from the south, over the bridge that had
been closed so long.

The British still held forts to the north of Orléans. But,
dispirited by the defeat of the southern garrisons, they resolved to withdraw. Sunday, May 8, the British put their
remaining forts to the torch, and drew up outside the city in
full battle array, as though to challenge the French defenders
to a final combat in the open.

Joan's generals were eager to continue the attack. Joan had
had enough of blood, though. A battle on Sunday was impossible. "In the name of God," she said, "let them depart,
and let us return thanks to God." Seeing that no battle was
forthcoming, the English withdrew.

The siege of Orléans was lifted. In but a week Joan had
driven off the English. The incredible news reverberated
through all France. The dauphin rejoiced. The English, dazed
by their defeat at the hands of this mere girl, muttered of
sorcery.

The English, falling back, occupied the towns of Meung,
Beaugency, and Jargeau. Joan drove them out one by one. On
May 13, she met the dauphin at Tours, and urged him to go

with her to Rheims to be crowned king. The angels had promised that she would save Orléans, and she had. Now the second part of her promise had to be fulfilled.

By June, the English had been driven out of Beaugency. They fell back to Patay; Joan drove them out. It became a rout. The English retreated, the French advanced. On July 16, Rheims opened its gates to the dauphin, and he knelt in the cathedral where France's kings had always been crowned.

Until this moment, the dauphin was only a self-proclaimed monarch. Now, thanks to Joan, he was the Lord's Anointed, Charles VII of France. It was more than a formality. The coronation assured Charles of the loyalty of all France, and no one could question his right to rule.

Joan now thought her mission had been accomplished, and she asked King Charles to dismiss her, to send her home to her village and her flocks. But Charles knew that his struggle was far from over. The English still held much of France, and he desperately needed Joan's aid to drive them out. She had an uncanny sixth sense that made her a better general than the generals, and the mere sight of her banner was enough to drive French troops into a frenzy of zeal and to strike English troops cold with terror.

Joan agreed to stay on, though her voices no longer spoke to her. She led the armies of France northward. Charles, ever weak, kept dreaming of a truce, but nothing less than complete victory would satisfy Joan. Certainly Paris had to be in Charles' hands before she could rest.

During the summer of 1429, she led the army from triumph to triumph, and by September they were at Paris. There, the English were still too strong, and the French attack was repulsed. Joan herself was again severely wounded.

A truce followed, and Joan chafed impatiently. In Easter week of 1430, Saints Catherine and Margaret told her that she would soon be captured, but despite this, learning that the

Duke of Burgundy was about to lay siege to Compiègne, she hastened to that city. On May 23, she rode out against the Burgundians, was separated from her men, and was captured.

The Burgundians promptly sold her to the English for 10,000 francs, and she was put on trial for sorcery. The English aim was to invalidate the coronation of Charles VII. If they could get the Church to declare Joan a witch, it would discredit Charles in the public eye, and leave the boy king of England, Henry VI, with a clear claim to the throne.

Joan was tried in January 1431. After long questioning she broke down and admitted, in May, that her "voices" had been of the Devil. Four days later, she recovered her self-confidence and repudiated her confession, but it was too late. She was taken to the marketplace at Rouen and burned at the stake, on May 29, 1431. Charles VII, whom she had given a throne, did not lift a finger to save her.

Joan was dead, but so, too, was the English attempt to conquer France. The turning point had been Orléans. Had it fallen, the dauphin would have fled, and France would have surrendered. Thanks to Joan, Orléans held out. Soon, the alliance between England and Burgundy foundered. In 1444, the English and the French, equally exhausted by the long war, agreed on a five-year truce, and when hostilities resumed, in 1450, the French, with revived strength, swept through Normandy and drove the descendants of William the Conqueror from the province. In October 1453, Bordeaux also fell to the French, and the English were expelled from France.

Joan of Arc, that strange girl, had by mystic and perhaps holy powers saved France from certain defeat. She inspired her people, and France emerged from the war a unified nation for the first time since the days of Charlemagne. Now the days of French greatness were to begin.

And if Orléans had fallen? England and France would have been under one rule, and neither country would have developed as it ultimately did. The rivalry between England and France over the next three centuries did much to spark the growth of both nations.

The spirit of Joan of Arc has served to guide France through hardship and turmoil for more than 500 years. The wrong done her by the British was remedied in 1456, when the "sorceress" verdict of 1431 was set aside by the Church. In 1920 Pope Benedict XV named Joan a saint—and, as Saint Joan, she shares heaven with the saints whose voices taught her how to save France.

CHAPTER EIGHT

THE BATTLE OF LEPANTO

Don John Smashes the Turks

IN 732 at Tours, Charles Martel had hurled the Arabs from Europe. But the Moslem threat remained. The Arabs themselves quarreled internally and lost control of their empire, but new converts to Islam, the Ottoman Turks, took their place as the rulers of the Moslem world.

Through the twelveth and thirteenth centuries, the Ottomans conquered most of the Near East, building an empire just as the Assyrians, the Persians, the Macedonians, and so many others had done in those countries before them. The Turks nibbled away at eastern Europe. Hungary, Albania, Greece, the places that are now called Rumania, Bulgaria, Yugoslavia—all became part of the Ottoman Empire. In 1453 Constantinople fell to the Turkish Sultan Mohammed II, ending the last vestige of the Roman Empire of the East. When Sultan Mohammed died, his empire stretched from the Danube east, and from the Black Sea to the Adriatic. All Europe feared the Turk. The divided, warring nations of Europe were menaced by the bold, united Ottoman thrust.

In western Europe, another Moslem stronghold had existed in Spain, where Arabs, not Turks, clung to power. By 1492, however, the Moors were expelled from Spain. A new Christian empire was forming.

The King of Spain, Ferdinand, died in 1516. His grandson Charles, already King of the Netherlands, succeeded him. And four years later Charles was offered the throne of the Holy Roman Empire, a confederation of Germanic states that traced its history to Charlemagne. As the Emperor Charles V, he ruled over all of Catholic Europe except Italy—and in 1530 he forced the Pope to give him Italy's crown. Spain, Austria, Germany, Italy, the Netherlands, all were united under the rule of Charles V. Charles now turned to deal with the Turk.

The Ottomans had not been idle. In 1526 they had made themselves masters of Hungary, and in 1529 their armies had come as far west as Vienna. They had failed to conquer, though, and had fallen back for the time being. Still, they controlled two-thirds of the Mediterranean, and Turkish ships menaced all the commerce of the Christian world.

In 1556 Charles laid down his many crowns and gave his throne to his son, who as Philip II would rule over all of Catholic Europe, most of the New World, and even—for a few years—England, since he was the husband of England's Queen Mary. Holding such a vast and unwieldy empire together was no simple matter. Philip was plagued with rebellion and strife in the Netherlands, in Spain, and in many other parts of his empire.

When Arab power in Spain had been broken, many of the Moors had agreed to become Christians. But inwardly they remained Moslem. In 1568, these Christianized Arabs, the

Moriscos, rebelled and massacred thousands of Spanish Christians. The Moriscos had sent an appeal to their fellow-Moslem, the Ottoman Sultan, for help.

Sultan Selim II was only too glad to lend aid. He had every reason to hate Philip, the most powerful monarch of the Christian world, and hoped that the rebellion in Spain would weaken the Christians enough to allow a further extension of Ottoman power. He offered his support to the Moriscos, and at the same time struck again at eastern Europe.

The island of Cyprus then was ruled by the Republic of Venice. Sultan Selim, in 1570, demanded that Venice surrender Cyprus to the Turks.

Venice turned to Europe for aid. But the Venetians were unpopular, partly because they were rich, and partly because they had long been friendly to the Turks. If the Turks wanted to turn on their Venetian allies, the other kings of Europe said, what worry is that of ours?

Only Pope Pius V saw that the Turks would not be content simply with Cyprus, but would move on to further conquest. In those days the Pope had military forces at his disposal. Pope Pius, eager to lead a crusade against the Turks, offered 12 warships to Venice, and persuaded Philip to divert his attention from Spain long enough to send aid to Venice as well.

Thus was born the Christian League. Its goal was to beat the Turks back, to drive them from Europe—or, at the very least, to keep them from moving any farther westward.

Throughout 1570 the Venetians on Cyprus desperately fended off the Turks while the League was being organized. The nations of Europe were in conflict over the purpose of the League, and over its control.

After long debate, Don John of Austria, half-brother of Philip II, was chosen supreme commander of the League. The other nations insisted, however, that Don John could not take any action without the consent of the leaders of every contingent in the League.

Don John was twenty-six in 1571. "His inspiring presence," one historian has written, "swept men off their feet, and made them temporarily forget their own selfish aims in an overwhelming enthusiasm for the common cause."

The Venetians were about ready to yield Cyprus when the League finally emerged from the council chambers. It was agreed that the various Catholic countries—which excluded Protestant England—would contribute a total of 200 galleys, 100 other warships, 50,000 infantry, 4,500 cavalry, and a large number of cannon. Half the expenses of the war would be met by Spain, with the other half divided two-thirds to Venice and one-third to the Pope. The other Catholic nations declined to join the League.

On June 20, Don John sailed from Spain to Italy, bringing with him a Spanish fleet. At Genoa, he added Italian ships, and proceeded on down the Italian coast, collecting ships and soldiers as he went. By August, he was at the port of Messina, where he was joined by Marco Antonio Colonna, commander of the papal contingent, and the seventy-five-year-old Sebastian Veniero, commander of the Venetian forces.

The Turks, meanwhile, continued to hammer Cyprus. They laid siege to the town of Famagusta, and took it in August, but only after suffering the loss of 50,000 men. They comforted themselves by committing frightful atrocities on the captured Venetian soldiers. With Cyprus fallen, the Turks planned to attack Venice herself. They sailed up the Adriatic and actually reached Venice, which was undefended. But then they learned that a huge allied fleet was assembled at Messina, which is on Sicily, just opposite the "toe" of the Italian "boot." Realizing they could be trapped if they remained in the Adriatic, the Turks quickly reversed themselves and headed for the island of Corfu, at the mouth of the Adriatic.

The Turks were driven from Corfu and moved on into the Gulf of Corinth. They dropped their anchor at the harbor of Naupactus. Naupactus is also known as Lepanto, and the Gulf of Corinth as the Gulf of Lepanto. "The Battle of Lepanto" is the name by which the ensuing struggle has always been called.

At Messina, Don John had assembled a formidable fleet: 300 ships, and 80,000 men, 30,000 soldiers and the rest seamen and galley slaves. Each nation in the armada wanted its own counsel to predominate, and Don John avoided bickering by reshuffling the ships so that every squadron held ships of Spain, ships of Venice, and ships of the Pope. In this way he created a truly international fleet. He arrayed it in three divisions, a center of 64 galleys under his own command, a right of 54 galleys, a left wing of 53, a rear guard of 30 galleys, and an 8-galley vanguard. Other types of ships—galleasses, frigates, and brigantines—were distributed through the three divisions.

General Fuller's description of these types of ships will make an understanding of the battle easier:

"The galley was a single-decked vessel varying from 120 to 180 feet in length, with a beam of about 20 feet and a depth of hold of 7; she was propelled by sail or oars, but in battle always by the latter, and for a short spurt could move at 6½ knots. The Christian galleys mounted five bow guns, the Turkish three. The former had also a number of 4½ pounders on each broadside; their planking was from three to four inches thick, and the rowers were protected by wooden mantlets, the Turkish were not. The galley was provided with a metal beak from 10 to 20 feet long. In rough weather she was an indifferent fighting vessel.

"The galleon was propelled by sails only; she was a large vessel rising from the waterline a third of her length, and with her two gun-decks was a floating fortress. Between the above two came the galleass, a ship half galley and half galleon, with lofty poop and forecastle, carrying from 50 to 70 pieces of ordnance, also four 20-barrel *ribaudequins* to cover the ship's waist against boarders. One of her main advantages over the galley was that she had a deck over her rowers. Her masts were lateen-rigged and her bows proof against cannon shot. The brigantine and frigate were small half-decked, two-masted vessels, moved by sails or oars."

On September 10, the leaders of the League gathered to form their plans. Some wanted immediately to pursue the Turks to Lepanto, others voted to wait. Don John was on the side of the attackers.

He knew that the League could not hold together indefinitely. National rivalries would eventually break it up if they waited without seeing action. But if they plunged into the fray, and attacked the Turks, the confederation would remain intact. To take the offense was the only course.

But it was a risky one. A wrong move, a Turkish victory, and all Europe would be helpless before the Turk. Don John's decision was an all-or-nothing gamble.

On September 29, Don John sailed eastward with his division. The rest of the ships remained behind, but only until Don John had learned the true size of the Turkish fleet awaiting him at Lepanto. Hurriedly he sent for the other ships under Veniero and Colonna. By October 3, the fleet was together again, and continued east, passing by Actium, where 1,600 years earlier Mark Antony had been humbled. Putting into harbor on October 5, they learned that Cyprus had fallen, and of the hideous fate that had befallen the garrison at Famagusta. The desire for revenge against the Turks kindled warlike spirits in Don John's armada.

The bickering between nations that Don John had feared nearly wrecked the expedition that same day. A Spanish officer aboard a Venetian galley got into a quarrel, and several men were killed. Veniero, the Venetian commander, promptly hanged the Spaniard without notifying Don John. Enraged at the news, Don John considered arresting Veniero, but Colonna, the commander of the papal forces, restored order and harmony. It was a bad sign, Don John felt. When even he could not resist losing his temper, how could the others stay cool?

The quarrel was patched up, and by October 7, after some bad weather, the fleet was on its way again. The Turks had word from scouts of Don John's approach. On October 6, they quitted Lepanto, boarded their ships, and moved to Galata, 15 miles west of Lepanto, where they rested overnight before continuing westward to meet the Christian fleet.

By daybreak on the 7th, the two fleets were only 10 miles apart, the Turks in the Gulf of Lepanto, the Christians just outside. When the first Turkish ships were sighted, Don John ordered the banner of the League hoisted, and the guns of his ship boomed out a signal that the battle was about to begin.

The commanders conferred aboard Don John's ship, the *Real*. Even now, some were opposed to the idea of doing battle so far from home base. Don John told them coolly, "Gentlemen, the time for counsel is past, and the time for fighting is come."

Don John drew up his three divisions in battle formation, the ships strung out over four miles of water. Aboard every ship, each man knelt in prayer, sunlight glittering on their mail as they bowed.

The Turks likewise divided their fleet in three. Ali Pasha, the commander, ordered the ships arrayed in a huge crescent stretching across the gulf from shore to shore. At half-past nine in the morning, Ali Pasha gave the order for the crescent to straighten out, forming a solid wall of ships across the gulf.

The Christian ships approached. Don John had placed a dozen big galleasses three quarters of a mile in front of his squadrons, and Ali Pasha was puzzled to see these powerful ships coming toward him. One of his lieutenants urged him to make a mock retreat, so as to draw the galleasses out of formation, just as the English were drawn at Hastings. Ali Pasha did not like the idea, though. He gave the order to advance. At half-past ten, the two fleets entered battle.

"Naval tactics in the Mediterranean," writes General Fuller, "consisted in maneuvering for position, followed by head-on assault in line abreast, outflanking and boarding, much as they had been at Salamis, Actium, and other ancient naval battles. To all intents and purposes, battles at sea were land battles fought on water."

The three Christian squadrons became separated. The left wing moved ahead, under Admiral Barbarigo, keeping clear of the shore for fear of shoals. On the right, Admiral Doria tried to keep pace with the left, but he was outmaneuvered by the Turks. The Turkish left wing extended past the Christian right wing, and Doria, fearing being outflanked and surrounded, was led into moving far out on a diagonal.

As a result, a mile-long gap opened between the Christian ring wing and Don John's squadron, in the center. While this was happening, the Christian left wing, under Admiral Barbarigo, was encountering the Turkish right wing, under Sirocco.

Barbarigo's galleasses opened fire with their heavy guns, and the Turks were thrown into confusion and were forced toward the shore. Barbarigo followed, and cut the Turks off from shore, then swung some of his ships around "like a closing door" to encircle them. Barbarigo himself was killed by a Turkish arrow, and for a while the Christians faltered, and matters grew worse when Barbarigo's nephew and second-in-command, Marco Contarini, also fell.

Another officer, Frederigo Nani, took charge and renewed the assault. The Turks were driven into the shore. They abandoned their galleys and took to their heels, hotly pursued by Venetian soldiers. The entire Turkish right wing thus was wiped out early in the battle.

Half an hour later, the two center divisions met. Again, the heavy fire of the Christian galleasses in the lead disrupted the Turkish ranks. The Turkish fire passed harmlessly over the Christian ships. The vessels met head-on, and twice Ali's men boarded Don John's flagship, only to be driven back, and twice Don John's men boarded Ali's ship. Fierce fighting continued for hours.

Then, just before one o'clock, the Christians boarded Ali's ship a third time. A musket shot struck the Turkish commander in the forehead and knocked him down; an instant later a swipe of a Spanish sword sent his head rolling. The Turkish flagship was taken, and the center of the Turkish fleet routed.

On the Christian right, however, all was not so well. Doria's squadron had been pulled out of position, creating a gap in the Turkish line, and now the Turkish left, under Uluch Ali, broke through between the Christian right and center. The Turks bore down on the Christian right wing and shattered it. Sir William Stirling-Maxwell, in his life of Don John, writes, "In the *Florence*, a Papal galley, not only many knights of St. Stephen were killed, but also every soldier and slave; and the captain, Tommaso de Medici, himself severely wounded, found himself at the head of only seventeen wounded seamen. In the *San Giovanni*, another vessel of the Pope, the soldiers were also killed to a man, the rowing-benches occupied by corpses, and the captain laid for dead with two musket-balls in his neck. The *Piamontesa* of Savoy had likewise lost her commander and all her soldiers and rowers."

The Turkish breakthrough, though, was speedily checked. The Marquis de Santa Cruz came up from the rear with his reserve fleet to attack Uluch Ali, and Don John, fresh from his victory over Ali Pasha in the center, also came to the rescue. Hastily, Uluch Ali and as many of his ships as still were able fled the scene.

It was an overwhelming victory for the Christian League. Don John had shown great skill in his superb use of the clumsy but deadly galleasses, and his handling of the various nationalities in his fleet showed military genius. Writes General Fuller:

"The age-old supremacy of the oar-propelled warship was at an end. Lepanto was the last of the great galley battles. . . . Henceforth sail and broadside fire were to replace oar and head-on attack."

Lepanto was a costly battle in human life. On the Christian side, 15,000 out of 84,000 men were killed or wounded, and among the wounded was one Miguel Cervantes, later to write *Don Quixote*. The Turks lost more than 30,000 out of 88,000, and thousands more were taken prisoners. The Christians captured many Turkish ships, hundreds of cannon, and vast sums of money that the Turks had been carrying.

Word of the victory electrified Christian Europe. In 1572, Pope Pius V, who had sparked the birth of the League, died, and the unity of the forces of Catholicism was lessened with his passing. That year, the Turks rebuilt their navy, but there was no further battle. Dissension in Europe broke up the League. The Venetians made peace with the Sultan, and Cyprus remained in Turkish hands.

Lepanto, like Marathon, was one of those battles whose importance was more symbolic than actual. Lepanto did not end the threat of the Turk to Europe. It did not even recover Cyprus. But it demonstrated that the nations of Europe, by acting in unison, could beat the Turk. For the first time since 1453, when Constantinople had fallen, Europeans began to believe that they might defeat the Turks after all. The Turkish conquest of Europe no longer seemed so inevitable. Lepanto was the first breach in the wall of Turkish confidence, and that first breach is often of critical importance. It was not until 1697 that the Turks were finally driven from central Europe, and forced to be content with the Balkan states and no more. But after Lepanto, the final defeat of the Ottomans was no longer a matter for doubt, and the people of Europe could sleep more soundly at night.

CHAPTER

NINE

THE DEFEAT OF

THE SPANISH ARMADA

ON July 19, 1588, the story goes, a bowling match was taking place at the English port of Plymouth. The bowlers were no ordinary men. They were England's finest heroes, the titans of her golden age.

Sir Walter Raleigh was there, and Sir Francis Drake, the first Englishman to sail around the world. Sir John Hawkins, a veteran of many battles; Sir Martin Frobisher, who boldly had led his fleet into the frozen waters of the Arctic in search of the Northwest Passage; Lord Howard of Effingham, England's high admiral; and many others of England's naval chiefs. In the harbor waited the fleet. An invasion was due. King Philip of Spain—the same ruler who had sent Don John to Lepanto 17 years before—planned to conquer England, depose Queen Elizabeth, and restore the British Isles to the roll of Catholic countries.

All spring it had been rumored that a great armada of

Spanish ships had assembled at Lisbon and would soon sail on England. The English admirals had planned to take to the sea, and meet the Spanish fleet in Spanish waters, but storms had driven them back to Plymouth. There they waited, and amused themselves on the bowling green.

And now word came! Spanish ships had been sighted off the Cornish coast! The Armada was on the way!

The English admirals, caught by surprise with their own fleet at anchor, were dismayed. They were all for rushing down to the ships at once.

Only Sir Francis Drake was cool. He knew that it was only three o'clock in the afternoon, and no ship could leave Plymouth until the tide changed, at ten that night. There was no hurry. He hefted his bowling ball and said calmly, "We have time enough to finish the game and beat the Spaniards too." And he turned his attention back to the ninepins.

The quarrel between Catholic Spain and Protestant England had been going on a long while. King Philip of Spain, master of half Europe and most of America, had married Mary, daughter of Henry VIII, who became Queen of England. When Mary died in 1558, Philip offered to marry her half-sister Elizabeth, the new queen. But Elizabeth, a Protestant, did not wish to marry Philip or any other man.

Until 1570 relations between Spain and England were reasonably friendly. Philip supported Elizabeth, mainly because Elizabeth's rival for the throne, Mary, Queen of Scots, was a potential danger to Philip's empire. But in 1568 Mary was imprisoned by Elizabeth and ceased to be a threat to Philip. Philip had no longer any reason for backing Elizabeth.

Friction between Spain and England developed over the matter of piracy. Spanish ships were bearing tons of gold from the New World—and also slaves from Africa. British privateers, quietly supported by Elizabeth, were intercepting these ships and making free with Spanish treasure.

Next, the Netherlands, part of Philip's empire, rebelled. The Dutch were Protestants, and Elizabeth supported them in their fight against Spain. Don John, the hero of Lepanto, was governor of the Netherlands, and he reported to his half-brother Philip, "The English queen is financing the revolt." He recommended war with England. This was in 1576.

The march of events was rapid. In 1577, Drake sailed around the world, looting the Spanish colonies of the New World on his way. In 1578, the Spanish attempted to invade Ireland, but failed, as they did again in 1580. In that same year Philip sent troops into Portugal and added that once-powerful kingdom to his own empire. But in the Netherlands, Holland and the six Northern Provinces made themselves independent of Spanish rule. And in 1585 Elizabeth sent 5,000 English soldiers to the aid of the rebels in Holland.

War was not far off. Philip saw that his only hope of regaining Holland was to conquer England as well. For years he had been shying back from so difficult a task. Now he had little choice but to plunge on toward war.

Elizabeth's roving sea captains were adding to Philip's miseries. Drake and Frobisher, in 1585, had ravaged the West Indies, from Florida to Colombia, at great cost to the Spanish. The slave trade from Africa was wholly disrupted.

In 1586, the Marquis of Santa Cruz, who had seen action at Lepanto, was given the assignment of gaining command of the English Channel. A Spanish fleet assembled, but the English learned of the plan. In April 1587, Drake set sail for the Spanish port of Cádiz, boldly entered the harbor, burned 32 Spanish ships and carried away four more. Next he made for Lisbon, cast terror into the Spanish, and destroyed 24 more ships. By June, he was back at Plymouth, having single-handedly wrecked most of the Spanish fleet with his whirlwind attack.

The surprise onslaught had saved England. The English

would not have been in a position to resist a full attack of the Spanish Armada in 1587. Drake's lightning swoop had evened the odds. Spain had to delay and rebuild. In Drake's phrase, he had "singed the king of Spain's beard."

By February 1588, Spain had built a new fleet. But its sailing was delayed by the death of the Marquis of Santa Cruz. This was a second blow to the Spaniards. Their most capable admiral was dead—Don John had died many years before—and in place of Santa Cruz, Philip named the Duke of Medina Sidonia, a nobleman with no military experience whatever, to command the new fleet.

Naval warfare had changed within the generation past, as we saw at Lepanto. The ancient idea of sinking an enemy ship by ramming her with the beak of your own had gone. Now cannon were mounted on every ship of war.

Philip knew that the English had better guns and better marksmen. So when he planned strategy for the invasion with Medina Sidonia, he pointed out that the English would try to conduct the battle at long range, where their guns would be effective and the Spanish guns would not. Philip warned Medina Sidonia, "The object of our side should be to close and grapple and engage hand in hand."

But there were other differences between the Spanish and the English fleets besides the efficiency of their cannon. The Spanish ships were top-heavy with soldiers, and the poor creatures who sailed them were treated almost like slaves. The English ships were staffed with capable sailors who were paid well, and could fight well beyond their naval skills. Thus the English ships could handle themselves in poor weather. The undermanned Spanish ships could not.

While the Spanish assembled their new armada, Drake and the other English admirals urged Queen Elizabeth to give the order for attack. Elizabeth hesitated. She still hoped for peace without a battle. Philip had sent negotiators to discuss peace, but this was only a ruse to give him time to prepare. Elizabeth fell into the trap. If the advice of Drake had been followed, the Armada would have been wiped out a second time before it could leave Spain. But the English ships remained in port. Drake warned her, "We are losing our advantage. We must attack them in their own waters."

All spring Elizabeth held back, while rumors came from Spain that the Armada was about to sail. In mid-May, it actually did sail, but had hardly cleared the coast of Spain before it was driven back by a violent storm, with many losses. On hearing this, Drake was able to get permission to carry the attack to Spanish waters, to seize what he called "the advantage of time and place." On May 30, the English fleet put to sea but it, too, was forced back. A second attempt, on June 24, also met with failure.

The English fleet returned to Plymouth. Meanwhile, on July 12, the Armada set sail once again, despite the continuing stormy weather, and this time succeeded in forcing passage. A week later, on the 19th, while the famous game of bowls was taking place at Plymouth, an English vessel in the Channel sighted the Spanish fleet, and hurried to Plymouth to bring the news.

The English had been caught in their own waters. "The advantage of time and place" had fallen to Spain. But it was not a complete surprise. Though at anchor, the English fleet was in a state of readiness for war. At nightfall on the 19th, as the tide changed, the royal galleons of England pulled out of Plymouth Sound, and the following morning headed to sea.

King Philip had ordered Medina Sidonia to keep to the French side of the Channel until a second fleet, under the Duke of Parma, could join forces with his. But the hope of destroying the English fleet at Plymouth had brought Medina Sidonia close to the English coast. Now, as Admiral Howard led the fleet out, the Spanish drew back.

On Saturday, July 20, the two fleets met. The Spanish were drawn up in a crescent seven miles from horn to horn—about 130 ships, half of them ships of war. The English fleet numbered 90. The first attack was little more than a skirmish, and a few Spanish ships were captured. The Spanish were astonished by the speed and power of the English fleet. Medina Sidonia wrote, "The enemy's ships were so fast and handy that there was nothing which could be done with them."

The Armada fell back to regroup and reconsider. Drake, in his ship the *Revenge*, gave chase and captured the treasure-laden vessel of Don Pedro de Valdéz, an important Spanish leader.

Calm seas prevented further action for a few days. Both fleets sat motionless, almost within cannonshot range of each other. The early skirmishes had seen the Spanish fare poorly, but there had been no real test of strength yet. By Friday, July 26, the Spanish had fallen back nearly to the French coast. Their fleet numbered only 124, now. The English, bolstered by late reinforcements, now had 136 ships, 46 of them "great ships." And the English had fresh stores of ammunition; the Spanish were already running low. The expected Spanish reinforcements under the Duke of Parma had not arrived.

Medina Sidonia landed at Calais and sent a messenger to the duke. He returned with news that the duke could not embark for two more weeks at the very least; his fleet was blockaded by Dutch ships to the north. It was discouraging news.

On the night of July 28, the English drew near the anchored Spanish fleet and sent fireships among them—unmanned hulks ablaze from stem to stern. As the fireships drifted toward the Armada, the Spanish panicked. Hastily they cut cables and headed to sea. In the darkness and confusion many of the Spanish ships collided and were damaged.

The fireships themselves did no damage. But with great ease the English had driven the Armada from its safe anchorage and out to sea in the dark. By morning, the Spanish ships were scattered all up and down the French coast. The full English fleet now bore down on the disorganized Armada.

The battle lasted from nine that morning to six at night. The English kept to the windward and fired deadly broadsides from long range. A Spanish observer wrote, "The English . . . discharging their cannons marvelously well . . . we were on so nigh another and they a good space asunder one from the other. . . . This day was slain Don Philip de Cordova with a bullet that struck off his head, and 24 men that were with us trimming our foresail. . . ."

It seemed as though the Armada might be totally destroyed that day. Ship after Spanish ship went down under the relentless pounding of the English guns. The Spanish, unable to carry out their favorite tactic of coming to close quarters and boarding, were helpless.

Toward nightfall, though, a squall came up. By then the English had all but exhausted their ammunition anyway, and had to withdraw. To add to the Spanish losses, the storm that night drove three ships onto the coast.

Tuesday, July 30, dawned grimly for the battered Armada. Medina Sidonia awoke to find 109 English ships less than two miles astern. His own fleet was widely dispersed, and a strong northwest wind was driving them toward the coast of Europe. They stood in only six fathoms of water now. They would soon be aground if the wind failed to change.

For once luck favored Spain. The wind changed to a southwester and they were able to avoid the shore. Quickly they ran north and assembled once again, their ranks greatly thinned by the disastrous battle the day before.

The Spanish admirals conferred to see if the Armada could somehow be saved. The problem now was returning to Spain.

They had been driven through the English Channel and into the North Sea.

"If the wind changes," Medina Sidonia decided, "we'll sail south and attempt to force our way back through the Channel. If the wind remains as it is, we'll continue north."

The wind did not change. The Armada was forced to continue north and take the long way home, around Scotland and down the Atlantic west of Ireland.

The English gave chase. To Sir Francis Drake fell the honor of pursuing the fleeing Spaniards. He sped northward as far as the Firth of Forth, in Scotland. But the English fleet's provisions were running low, and their ammunition all but expended—expended to good effect, but all the same gone. And now it seemed that the dazed Spaniards were abandoning the Scottish coast and heading vaguely toward Norway. Drake decided that it was best to abandon the chase, and, as he put it, "to leave them to those boisterous and uncouth northern seas." In the first week in August, the victorious but hungry English turned back.

There was still one hope for Spain. Scotland had no love for England, ever since Queen Elizabeth had put to death her rival, Mary Queen of Scots. If Medina Sidonia and the remnants of the Spanish Armada had landed in Scotland, they could have raised a rebellion and swept down toward England at the head of an angry army.

Medina Sidonia's only concern, though, was getting home. He had had enough of warfare for a while. The one-sided slaughter of his Armada had left him with no taste for fighting the English.

The worst part of his campaign still lay ahead of him, however. The journey home was even more dreadful than the guns of the English. The galleass *Girona* went to pieces first, buffeted by the wind off Ireland's Giant's Causeway. The *El Gran Griffon* went down in a storm off Fair Island. On the coast of Erris, the *Rata Coronada* was wrecked. Glennagiveny Bay was the burial ground of the *Duquesa Santa Ana.* Fierce winds blew other ships far off course, even to the shores of England, where they sank. All down the Irish coast the Spanish galleons perished at the hands of wind and storm—*San Juan, Triniada, Valencera, San Marcos, Señora de la Rosa,* all the proud warships of Spain.

The lucky Spaniards were those who went down with their ships. They met swift deaths. Others scrambled ashore in Ireland and were gleefully murdered by the half-wild Irish. (A few survived and married Irish maidens, though, and their descendants, with their Latin look, can still be seen in parts of Ireland.) Those Spaniards who were not butchered by the Irish died of starvation, or exposure, or untended wounds.

It was not until the middle of September that the surviving ships of the Armada staggered home. Sir Edward Creasy writes, "The sufferings and losses which the unhappy Spaniards sustained in their flight round Scotland and Ireland are well known. Of their whole Armada only fifty-three shattered vessels brought back their beaten and wasted crews to the Spanish coast which they had quitted in such pageantry and pride."

King Philip took the news remarkably well, all things considered. A messenger from the port of Santander, where Medina Sidonia had landed on September 12, came to him bearing the ill tidings.

Philip remarked philosophically, "Great thanks do I render Almighty God, by whose generous hand I am gifted with such power, that I could easily, if I chose, place another fleet upon the sea."

Philip was right in that the defeat of the Armada did not mean the immediate defeat of Spain. He did indeed place another fleet on the sea, and the war between Spain and England continued another fifteen years, until in 1603 both sides called it off by mutual consent with little gained for either. Nor did the defeat of the Armada end the Spanish command of the seas. Garrett Mattingly, in his book, *The Armada,* notes that "In fact, more American treasure reached Spain in the years between 1588 and 1603 than in any other fifteen years in Spanish history."

In what way, then, was the defeat of the Armada one of the decisive battles of history? It does not even seem to have been much of a contest. The English, with their strategy of keeping to the windward and fighting at long range, out-maneuvered the Spaniards under the inexperienced Medina Sidonia completely, so completely that the English did not lose a single ship during the whole encounter. The Spanish went from blunder to blunder, had their formations broken repeatedly, and ended by succumbing as much to the foul weather as to the English cannon.

And even if the Armada had successfully invaded England, would England have fallen? Professor Mattingly thinks not. The English would have defended their land valiantly against the Spanish invaders.

Then why decisive?

There were two reasons. First, it showed the world that the Spanish could be stopped. As Professor Mattingly remarks, "France and Germany and Italy had seen the Spanish colossus advance from victory to victory. Providence, God's increasingly obvious design, the wave of the future, seemed to be on the side of Spain, and, as Catholics, French and German and Italian Catholics rejoiced that Spain was clearly the elected champion of God's Church, little as they relished the prospect of Spanish dominance, while Protestants everywhere were correspondingly alarmed and dismayed. . . ." The outcome of the conflict, Mattingly feels, showed the Protestant peoples that God was, after all, on their side, and indicated to the Catholics of France, Italy and Germany that Spain "was not, after all, God's chosen champion. From that time forward, though Spain's preponderance was to last for more than another generation, the peak of her prestige had passed."

A seemingly minor event can have enormous consequences in a nation's history, and prestige is all important. Consider the changed position of the United States since that day in October 1957, when the first Russian sputnik soared into orbit. The launching of that satellite struck a mighty blow at the then universally held idea that the United States was the mightiest power on earth.

So, too, in the sixteenth century, the defeat of the Armada rocked Spain's prestige. Spain had built a mighty ocean-spanning empire on the concept of being God's chosen conquerors. The defeat of the Armada, General Fuller declares, "shattered this faith and destroyed the illusion that had fortified their fanaticism. Thirty years later Spain became decadent, not because the war with England had been long and exhausting, but because the loss of faith in her destiny was catastrophic."

There was a second decisive result to the encounter. England learned the true nature of her own strength: that it lay in her navy. A small country with limited resources, she could not muster mighty armies. But so long as she built ships and manned them with bold admirals and valiant sailors, she could have command of the sea, and thus of the world.

The torch of empire was once again passing. Spain's glittering day was almost over, and her long descent beginning. The small, determined nation of Englishmen would soon build an empire that stretched around the globe, on every continent, and they would found that empire on the strength of sea power. The defeat of the Armada gave England an unshakeable faith in her own ability to withstand an invader, a faith that has endured to this day.

THE BATTLE OF BLENHEIM

French Power is Checked

T HE seventeenth century was a time of troubles for Europe. While the German-speaking countries tore one another apart in the Thirty Years' War, England was sundered by civil strife, and her king was put to death by her people. By 1661, however, the monarchy had been restored in England, and the wounds of the Thirty Years' War were beginning to heal.

In that year of 1661 a young man of twenty-three came to power in France—Louis XIV, whose reign was to be marked by splendor and grandeur. Actually, Louis had been king since the age of five, in 1643. But throughout his boyhood his chief minister, Cardinal Mazarin, had been the real ruler of France. In 1661 Mazarin died and the young king took control himself.

Louis' dream was a Europe united under French sway, as it had been 800 years before in the days of Charlemagne. In 1667 French troops conquered the Spanish Netherlands (now

Belgium), and in 1672 turned on Holland as well. A three-cornered war followed, with England allied first with France against the Dutch, then withdrawing from the war. In 1678 it ended, and as part of the complicated peace settlement the Dutch possessions of New Amsterdam and New Jersey passed into English hands.

France continued to expand at the expense of her neighbors. Louis XIV, a Catholic, practiced a policy of persecuting Protestants. In 1685 Catholic James II came to the English throne, but he was driven out three years later, and William of Orange, a Dutchman and a Protestant, was given the crown. Louis XIV supported the exiled James II against William, and battle lines began to form in Europe once again. It would be England versus France in this new conflict.

Louis waged war against the German states, and William seized this opportunity to create a Grand Alliance against France. Austria, the Netherlands, England, the various German states—all joined against France in 1701. French aggression had to be checked. France had become the most powerful state in Europe, and the Protestant nations feared her greatly.

Ten days after the Grand Alliance was formed, James II, England's exiled king, died in France. Louis XIV promptly recognized his son James as James III, rightful King of England, and to add to the insult prohibited British goods from entering France. Britain promptly planned to go to war. But while the army was being assembled, William was thrown from his horse and died of injuries. His sister-in-law, Princess Anne, a daughter of James II, became England's queen.

It was a time of crisis for the Grand Alliance. William, its leader, was dead, and England now was ruled by an unremarkable and none too intelligent woman. Louis XIV, reigning in unparalleled majesty, was the dominant figure of Europe, and it seemed as though the Alliance would go to pieces. But Queen Anne announced her intention to continue William's

policies. And the Alliance was lucky to have as its command-
ing general one of the supreme military geniuses of English
history, the Duke of Marlborough.

Marlborough's career had been a stormy one. He had
changed sides several times in the struggles between James II
and William for the English crown, and he had now and then
been accused of treason. Whatever his personal failings, no
one doubted his military skill. General Fuller says of him, "As
a general he possessed the rare virtue of seeing a war as a
whole, and of being able to relate sea power with land power
and strategy with politics. Nothing escaped his observation,
and no detail, tactical or administrative, was too minute to be
overlooked. A master of strategems, he consistently mystified
his enemy; a master of detail, his men were never left in want.
In the planning of a campaign he took infinite pains, and in its
execution infinite trouble. In an age which believed that the
defensive was the stronger form of war, he invariably sought
to bring his enemy to battle, and proved conclusively that a
vigorous offensive is usually the soundest defense."

This was the man, daring, imaginative, bold, whom the
Grand Alliance chose to halt Louis XIV's conquest of Europe.
He fully understood the use of the new weapons of war—the
rifle and the bayonet. With a master's skill he divided and
arrayed his troops so that platoons firing in close range would
throw the enemy into confusion, and then a charge with
bayonets would complete the rout.

War was declared on May 15, 1702. On one side was
France and its ally Spain, supported by several of the rulers of
the many Italian kingdoms. On the other, England and the
Netherlands formed the western half of the Grand Alliance,
Austria the eastern, with neutral German states in between.
Marlborough's double task was to keep the Netherlands from
being invaded by the French, and to prevent a joint French
and Spanish army from taking Austria.

Nothing decisive occurred during the war's first two years. The rival armies prodded one another, exchanged victories, and accomplished little, except that the French moved into firm possession of neutral Bavaria, cutting the Alliance's lines of communication in two.

Marlborough had been fighting in the Netherlands, where matters had become stalemated. He saw that the French thrust into Germany threatened the safety of Vienna. If Austria fell, as now looked quite likely, the Alliance would be severely crippled. Marlborough conceived a bold plan: to march clear across Europe, through the heart of French territory, from Antwerp to the Upper Danube, and come to the aid of Vienna.

It was risky in the extreme. But Marlborough set out, on May 19, 1704. He led an army of 16,000 English troops, and added Dutch divisions as he went. The march was hampered by disagreements among the various leaders of the Allies, but Marlborough remained serene, kept the factions of the army together, and continued.

The French were bewildered. Where was Marlborough going? What did he hope to gain by abandoning the Netherlands? Surely he didn't plan to march all the way to Austria— so what was his plan, then? Where would he attack?

The French were unable to believe Marlborough was actually doing anything so fantastic as taking his army to the Danube. So, in their confusion, they held back, letting him pass, and by early summer Marlborough was at the Rhine.

The French now decided that he planned to invade Alsace, and assembled an army of 45,000 men to fight him there. Marlborough thoughtfully encouraged this idea. He had his men build a bridge across the Rhine as though he intended to enter Alsace. This tied up an entire army of Frenchmen uselessly—and Marlborough left the Rhine in June and continued on toward the Danube.

In early July he swept into Bavaria and drove out the

invaders everywhere but in the fortified cities of Munich and Augsburg. By this time, the French realized what was happening, and began to unite their scattered, confused armies near Augsburg to repel the Allies.

By August 12, an immense French army was massed near the village of Blenheim, in Bavaria, on the left bank of the Danube, under the command of Marshal Camille Tallard. Marlborough's army had joined with that of Prince Eugene of Austria and occupied a position a little to the west.

The French, who had been baffled by Marlborough's movements all summer, finally felt confident of victory. Their army was clearly superior in numbers. It would be suicide for Marlborough to attack. By all the rules of war, Marlborough would have to retreat and yield all he had won in the past two months.

But Marlborough did not obey the rules. He studied the situation. The French camp was atop a low hill. They were in a strong defensive position, flanked on one side by the Danube, on the other by woodland and hills. Their army numbered about 60,000, Marlborough's some 52,000.

Marlborough resolved to attack.

Early in the morning of August 13, the combined armies of Marlborough and Prince Eugene began to steal westward through the darkness and mist. By six o'clock in the morning, they had reached the high ground at Wolperstetten, to the north of the French camp.

The mist broke at seven, and the flabbergasted French rubbed their eyes and stared at the armies of Marlborough and Eugene just above their camp. Did Marlborough mean to attack after all?

Marshal Tallard thought not. "This is just a diversionary measure," he insisted. "They have sent a few divisions to distract our attention while their main body of troops withdraws." He was so confident that he sent a message off to

Louis XIV, informing him that Marlborough had decided to retreat.

If it was a retreat, though, it was a retreat in reverse. Marlborough's troops advanced toward the French in a menacing way that abruptly did not seem at all like a mere "diversionary measure." This was an attack.

A French historian, collecting eyewitness reports a few years later, wrote, "Signal guns were fired to bring back the foragers and their escorts; the 'Alarm' and the 'Assembly' were beaten hurriedly, and, without attempting to strike the tents, every effort was devoted to forming line of battle in front of the camp.

"The hurry and precipitation of all this brought confusion and fear in its train, whilst the foraging parties and their escorts, alarmed by the unexpected signals, returned one by one, rather a prey to misgivings than animated with any desire to fight. The difficulty of having to think of many things at once in the actual presence of the enemy reacted upon the nerves of those in command, and, above all, upon those who had their carriages packed with the valuables accumulated during their period of winter quarters."

The surprised French hurriedly formed a battle line. Tallard's army was actually, like Marlborough's, two armies—a French army, and a Bavarian one under the Elector of Bavaria. Tallard distributed his troops between the Danube on the right and the village of Lutzingen on the left. He himself took command of the right wing, Marshal Marsin of France the center, and the Elector the left wing. The right wing was much the strongest of the three. A stream called the Nebel ran from east to west between Marlborough's armies and Tallard's, and Tallard hoped to keep the enemy from crossing the stream on the right, while Marlborough's left would be allowed to cross and then cut down by fire on both sides and a cavalry charge in front.

Marlborough, with his talent for the unpredictable, devised a brilliant scheme for attack. The French would not expect an attack on their strong right wing. Therefore Marlborough would do just that. While Prince Eugene attacked the enemy left, Marlborough would concentrate his attention on the strongest part of Tallard's force.

The right wing, under Prince Eugene, had to march over rough ground. Marlborough drew up the left and center wings in front of the villages of Unterglau and Blenheim, and waited for Eugene to catch up. The morning passed. Marlborough sent a column under Lord Cutts to clear the French away from the left bank of the Nebel, but the real battle could not begin until Eugene arrived.

For four hours the opposing armies fired volleys at long distance. To keep up morale while his army waited for the Austrians, Marlborough rode down the lines in full view of the French artillery. At one point a shot struck the ground at the feet of the duke's horse, and for a moment he disappeared in a cloud of dust, and a worried cry went up.

But Marlborough was unharmed. At eleven, worried about Eugene's lateness, he sent off messengers. Frank Taylor, in his book *The Wars of Marlborough*, writes, "The sun shone brilliantly on acres of yellow grain, slashed with long, glittering lines of scarlet, blue and steel. The music of both armies rose and fell in challenging paeans. And always the cannon boomed across the marshy stream, and men and horses were cut down, now singly, and now in swathes, and the dismal procession of wounded trailed slowly to the rear. The heat became intense, for it was now high noon. The day was half spent, and already the casualties of the allies amounted to 2,000, when an aide-de-camp of Eugene's came racing from the distant right. The moment had arrived."

The time was 12:30. Marlborough nodded to his officers. "Gentlemen, to your posts."

Lord Cutts, leading part of Marlborough's left wing, attempted an attack on the village of Blenheim. A third of the foremost British brigade perished, but Cutts advanced again, and a second time was thrown back, with even heavier losses. Marlborough decided against a third attempt. Blenheim could not be taken, but at least the French soldiers defending it were removed from the battle, since they had to remain penned up in the village.

In the center, the French were falling back. The first line of Marlborough's infantry was already across the Nebel and the cavalry was beginning to cross, though encountering stiff resistance from Tallard's cavalry. Off to the allied right, Eugene and the Elector of Bavaria were clashing, with heavy losses on both sides.

At three in the afternoon, it seemed as though the French were prevailing. Marlborough's center was making little headway, Eugene was stopped completely, and time was passing. If the allies failed to break through Tallard's line, they would have no choice but to withdraw.

But Marlborough sensed his pathway to victory. Much of the French infantry was bottled up in the garrisons at Blenheim and Oberglau. If he could hold them there—and if Prince Eugene could maintain at least a stalemate to the right —it would be possible to smash through Tallard's gradually weakening line.

By four, Marlborough was ready for his master stroke. He had managed to bring the whole center of his army through the marshes of the Nebel, and Eugene was still hanging on at his right. The French were compelled to remain at their widely separated positions, and there was no way of reinforcing Tallard. Suddenly the relative strengths of the two armies had changed. Marlborough had been able to concentrate the bulk of his troops at one point, while Tallard's army was dispersed over a broad front.

At half-past four came the good news that Prince Eugene was pressing forward successfully at last. Marlborough arrayed his troops with the cavalry in the fore, and himself led the charge. In perfect order 8,000 horsemen thundered down on the fatigued army of Tallard, while battalions of allied infantry followed behind.

Furious French fire failed to drive the cavalry back. They crested the hill and smashed forward. The French cavalry, thrown into dismayed confusion, wheeled and took to flight, exposing nine French infantry battalions who were ridden down by the high-stepping attackers. Tallard and Marsin, the two French marshals, were cut off from one another by this thrust of allied cavalry.

"With trumpets blaring and kettledrums crashing and standards tossing proudly above the plumage and the steel," Taylor writes, "the two long lines, perfectly timed from end to end, swung into a trot, that quickened ever as they closed upon the French."

The nine French battalions of infantry were killed to the last man. Tallard gave the order for withdrawal, but by then his force was in full flight anyway. Tallard was taken prisoner; hundreds of his men were driven back into the Danube and drowned.

Prince Eugene was now forcing Marsin's army toward Marlborough. Marsin contrived a retreat that saved himself and some of his men, but left others defenseless and open to slaughter. By nine, the battle was over. The Allies had lost 4,500 men, and 7,500 more had been wounded. The total French and Bavarian casualties numbered 38,609, including prisoners. "The military ascendancy of the arms of the Allies was completely established," Creasy comments. "Throughout the rest of the war Louis fought only in defence. Blenheim had dissipated for ever his once proud visions of almost universal conquest."

The results of the Battle of Blenheim are complex and cannot easily be summarized, except to say that the battle put a permanent check to the French dream of a European empire. Fuller writes, "It broke the prestige of the French armies and plunged them into disgrace and ridicule." The power of England was greatly increased at France's expense. In Germany, a complete rearrangement of power would have resulted had Marlborough lost, and France would have emerged dominant in the German states.

Marlborough went on from triumph to triumph, and is remembered to this day as one of England's greatest heroes. A grateful nation built a lordly palace for the duke near Woodstock, in Oxfordshire. His descendants still occupy it—Blenheim Palace, it is called, in memory of the famous battle which, a biographer of the duke has rightly written, "changed the political axis of the world."

The greatness of Marlborough is indicated in another passage by that same biographer:

"Until the advent of Napoleon no commander wielded such widespread power in Europe. Upon his person centered the union of nearly twenty confederate states. He held the Grand Alliance together no less by his diplomacy than by his victories. He rode into action with the combinations of three-quarters of Europe in his hand. . . . He was for six years not only the Commander-in-Chief of the Allies, but, though a subject, virtually Master of England."

The man who wrote those lines was perhaps prejudiced in favor of Marlborough, since he is one of the duke's descendants—and a man who himself, "though a subject," was for a time "virtually Master of England." For the family name of the Duke of Marlborough was John Churchill. And his biographer was the man who, in 1940, bore England through its darkest hour as prime minister—Winston S. Churchill, the many-times-great-grandson of the Duke of Marlborough.

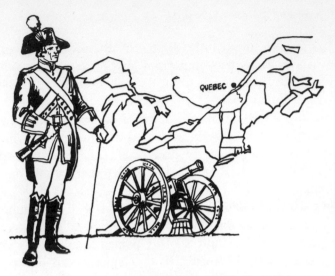

THE BATTLE OF
THE PLAINS OF ABRAHAM
The French Lose North America

THE struggles of the Old World were transplanted to the New. The rivalry between French and English flourished in the green new continent, until war became inevitable in the eighteenth century.

The English came to America as settlers. Jamestown, Plymouth, New York, Philadelphia—up and down the eastern seaboard, they built towns that grew rapidly. The French came as hunters and trappers, and as missionaries. They ranged through the wild north and central regions of the continent, slaughtering beavers and converting puzzled Indians to Christianity. By 1748, there were a million English colonists in North America, and only a tenth as many French.

In the middle of the eighteenth century, the French decided to expand their colonial empire. Governor de la Gallisonière of Canada studied the North American map and ran his finger down the thin strip of English colonies hugging the coast, then pointed inland, to the Ohio valley.

"If we plant colonies here," he murmured, "and build forts linking Canada with our colony in Louisiana, the English will be boxed in."

To counter this threat to their own expansion, the English had to build inland forts of their own. So in 1753, Governor Dinwiddie of Virginia sent a young officer named George Washington to build a fort at the confluence of the Allegheny and Monongohela rivers. But he was driven off, and the French built a fort on the site instead—Fort Duquesne.

In 1775 the British government decided to come to grips with the French. British soldiers—redcoats—were sent to America under General Braddock. They marched on Fort Duquesne and were slaughtered in ambush, since Braddock understood nothing about forest warfare. A formal declaration of war followed, in May 1756. The two contestants gathered their strength. England and France would fight for the possession of North America.

The French commander was a small, intense, vehement man named Louis Joseph, Marquis de Montcalm. The English general with whom Montcalm's name is forever linked is Brigadier General James Wolfe, who at the age of thirty-two was placed in command of the English forces in Canada, though older and more experienced generals were available.

Overall English strategy was dictated by that brilliant and controversial statesman, William Pitt the Elder, who had come from England to direct the war at close range. Pitt's aim was first to capture the important French forts near English territory, and then to move on to take French-held Canada, thus driving the French from all America but Louisiana.

In July 1758, the English under Wolfe and Jeffrey Amherst took Louisbourg, the French fort on the St. Lawrence River at Grand Breton Island. In November, the English drove the French from Fort Duquesne and renamed it Fort Pitt. We know it today as Pittsburgh.

The third English campaign of 1758 was less successful. In a disastrous attack on Ticonderoga, on Lake George, where the French had captured England's Fort William Henry two years before, 2,000 soldiers were lost. But this defeat was atoned for when a small English force under Colonel Bradstreet crossed Lake Ontario into Canada and burned Fort Frontenac. The French grip on Canada was weakening. As 1758 ended, Pitt resolved to attempt a broad attack on Canada in the new year.

It was now that James Wolfe came to his brief moment of fame. He was picked to lead the main land assault on the French stronghold of Quebec, while an English fleet attacked simultaneously by sea, and while Jeffrey Amherst diverted the attention of the French by again attacking Ticonderoga.

The appointment of a young general like Wolfe startled some British leaders. The Duke of Newcastle, who was the head of the British government at the time, hurried in amazement to King George II when he heard that Pitt had chosen Wolfe.

"The man must be mad!" Newcastle sputtered.

"Mad, is he?" the king is said to have replied. "Then I hope he will bite some others of my generals!"

Wolfe's appointment was confirmed. The young general had an even younger staff; all his subordinate commanders were under thirty. "It was a campaign of boys," one historian noted.

Wolfe had been in England on sick leave. In February 1759, he sailed for America. Pitt's plan was well designed: Wolfe to lead the main attack; Amherst to create a diversion; Admirals Saunders and Holmes to mount a naval attack on Quebec while Wolfe took it by land; and Admiral Durell to blockade the St. Lawrence River and keep French reinforcements from reaching Quebec.

Montcalm at first expected the main attack to come from Amherst, in the west, and he strengthened his lines along Lake Champlain and at Fort Niagara. The French general was hampered not only by the small force at his disposal, but by the dishonesty of the French officials in Canada, who gave him little cooperation. Montcalm was not even on speaking terms with the Marquis of Vaudreuil, the new governor of Canada. The disgusted Montcalm, surveying the situation, wrote, "Everybody appears to be in a hurry to make his fortune before the colony is lost; which event many perhaps desire as an impenetrable veil over their conduct."

Despite this discouraging attitude, Montcalm loyally vowed to save French Canada if at all he could. And good fortune appeared to be riding with him.

First, the blockade under Admiral Durell failed. The English fleet held back, afraid of the ice in the St. Lawrence, and a French squadron slipped through to Quebec with reinforcements. Aboard one of these ships was carried a letter from Amherst, intercepted at sea, which gave away the entire British plan. That was Montcalm's second stroke of luck.

He lost no time regrouping his troops for the defense of Quebec. He had about 12,000 men—a thousand of them Indians, many of the rest an almost untrained local militia. Against him was coming Wolfe's army of nearly 9,000 professionals, and a fleet of 170 ships, 18,000 seamen.

Geography favored the defenders. Quebec is high on a hill overlooking the St. Lawrence. Montcalm felt that time was on his side. If he could dig in and withstand a British onslaught from June till October, the coming of winter's fogs and gales would drive the British away.

Montcalm's strategy, therefore, was completely defensive.

He threw up a line of forts and earthworks as far as Mont-morency, seven miles northeast of Quebec on the St. Lawrence. He sent his ships upstream to keep them out of harm's way. In case the British got past the fortifications at Montmorency, 106 guns protected Quebec. The French dug in, working desperately to make their position impregnable.

The British assembled at Louisbourg in May and planned their attack. It was decided that the fleet would sail right up the St. Lawrence, something that had never been attempted before for fear of fog and rapids. Wolfe planned to launch his attack at Beauport, which lay midway between Quebec and Montmorency, and march southwest to attack Quebec from the rear.

The British fleet navigated the river without harm. The fog dangers turned out to have been greatly exaggerated, and the fleet, which had left the Atlantic on June 9, reached the Isle of Orleans, opposite Beauport, on June 26. Wolfe studied the position and realized at once that his original plan would never do. Beauport, like the rest of the west bank of the river from Montmorency to Quebec, was too well fortified. There was no way of storming the heights. It meant crossing open mud flats while French guns showered down a hail of death.

While Wolfe hesitated at the Isle of Orleans, the French sent seven fireships downstream toward them. The ships were loaded with rockets, bombs, grenades, and barrels of explo-sives, but the French set them off too soon, and the fireships did no damage. They created a fine fireworks spectacle for the British on the pitch-black night.

Wolfe now decided to force the attack on two fronts at once. He would occupy Point Lévis, directly opposite the city to the south, at a place where the river was less than a mile across, and shell Quebec from there. At the same time he would capture the high ground east of the Falls of Montmorency, and attempt to work westward toward Quebec from that direction.

On June 30 the British occupied Point Lévis easily and set up batteries there. Wolfe left Monckton, one of his three young brigadiers, in charge there and, leaving another small detachment to protect the British base on the Isle of Orleans, sent his other two brigadiers, Murray and Townshend, east of Montmorency.

Montcalm was in a serious predicament. The English guns at Point Lévis were doing heavy damage to the outskirts of Quebec, and he had to keep a detachment of his own men on the spot to forestall a possible landing there. Meanwhile, seven miles to the east, the British were menacing Montmorency. And food was running low in Quebec. Montcalm's badly trained militia was unruly and restless, and some of the men were deserting.

Still, Montcalm knew he had a chance, if only he could hold out until winter. He continued to play a waiting game, holding off the English as best he could on both fronts.

Wolfe feinted here, feinted there, but his coy maneuvers failed to fool Montcalm. The French stayed within their forts and refused to be drawn out.

Wolfe knew he would have to make a direct frontal smash and hoped to break through. On July 31, he ordered an attack on the French forts at Montmorency. Wolfe moved ships up to provide a naval bombardment of the forts, hoping that as his infantry advanced over the mud flats, the French would come down out of the heights and give battle.

The attack was a fiasco. Instead of coming down, the French fled to the upper forts and picked off the British with rifle fire. Then Montcalm's Indian troops swooped down to scalp the wounded. The British lost 30 officers and 400 infantrymen, and losses would have been heavier except for a sudden downpour that wet the powder of the riflemen and ended the massacre. The British fell back in dismay.

Again Wolfe was forced to change his strategy. "They will not come out and fight," he realized. "Very well. We'll lay waste the countryside and starve them out!"

The British proceeded to raid the villages surrounding the French fortifications, burning farms and cutting off Quebec's already jeopardized food supplies. Wolfe believed that hunger would lead Montcalm's rabble of a militia to desert, leaving the city open to quick attack. The guns at Point Lévis continued to pound away, destroying the lower town and setting fire to the cathedral.

In the west, meanwhile, Amherst had driven the French out of Ticonderoga by July 26, and was ready to move eastward to assist Wolfe. To block Amherst's advance, Montcalm was forced to send his most capable officer, the Chevalier de Lévis, to Montreal. British ships went upstream to harass this force, and for a while Quebec was almost ignored as the center of the stalemated battle shifted to the westward.

Late in August, Wolfe fell ill. By August 29, he had recovered, and he called his three brigadiers together to discuss some way of forcing the issue. Time was running out. Only about eight weeks of good weather remained before fog and snow would set in.

All three junior officers had the same idea: to abandon the position at Montmorency and concentrate everything at Point Lévis, just south of Quebec, for one powerful thrust.

"If we land on the north shore," they pointed out, "Montcalm will have to fight us on our own terms." Such a thrust would separate the two French forces—the one in the west fighting Amherst, and the one in the east defending Quebec. It would force the French to meet Wolfe's forces in the open, finally, where the better British discipline would show its value.

This change of plan brought the situation back to the start, though. Where could a direct attack on Quebec be made? The city was built on a cliff, and was heavily fortified. Wolfe himself reconnoitered and found a cove called Anse du Foulon, a mile and a half west of the town. It was densely wooded and only thinly defended by the French. The problem was finding the cove in the dark—for the landing had to be made at night—and safely coming ashore despite a strong tide.

On September 11, the orders were posted: the troops were to assemble on the beach at five the next morning. By this time Wolfe had brought all his forces together at Point Lévis. Montcalm was aware of this troop movement, but, plagued by Amherst in the west, did not suspect that a direct attack on Quebec was in the wind.

Wolfe's final orders were posted on September 12. "A vigorous blow struck at this juncture may determine the fate of Canada," he told his troops. "The first body that gets on shore is to march directly to the enemy, and drive them from any little post they may occupy. . . . The officers and men will remember what their country expects from them, and what a determined body of soldiers inured to war are capable of doing against five weak battalions, mingled with disorderly peasantry."

As the tide began to ebb, about two in the morning on the night of the 12th, the flatbottom boats pushed off to drift downstream toward Anse du Foulon. As he drifted across the river, Wolfe recited Gray's *Elegy Written in a Country Churchyard*. Reaching the line, "The paths of glory lead but to the grave," he looked solemnly at his men and said, "Gentlemen, I would rather have written those lines than take Quebec tomorrow."

The current carried the boats close to the cliff, and a French sentry called out, *"Qui vive?"*—Who goes there?

The French had been expecting provision barges that night,

and Wolfe knew this. One of his officers called back, in French, *"France!"*

"What regiment?" came the challenge.

"The Queen's," the British officer replied.

His accent must have been a convincing one. The sentry let the boats pass. A few minutes later, farther downstream, a second sentry challenged them, and this time the same officer said, "We are the provision convoy. Quiet or the English will hear us!"

The second sentry was as gullible as the first. The British passed, and moments later approached the cove. The strong current took the lead boat a quarter of a mile too far downstream. The men pulled ashore and backtracked along the beach, then climbed the hill toward the small French outpost. The French were quickly overpowered and the British swarmed ashore in great number. By daybreak, 5,000 of Wolfe's troops had crossed the river, and had assembled on the Plains of Abraham, a broad, open field to the west of the city.

While this was happening, Montcalm was several miles east of Quebec, at Beauport. Word came to him during the night that boats had been seen on the river, but he took these for the expected provisions convoy. The main body of his troops was concentrated at Beauport to meet what had seemed to be an English attack the night before, but which had really only been a diversionary feint.

Daybreak revealed the British massed on the Plains of Abraham. The news was brought to Montcalm, and he immediately ordered his troops shifted westward to meet the threat. But he ran into difficulties, because he did not have absolute command over the French forces. Vaudreuil, the governor, refused to let Montcalm have the troops in the forts from Beauport to Montmorency. And Ramesay, the garrison commander of Quebec, allowed Montcalm to have only three field guns instead of the 25 he wanted. Both men insisted that this invasion was only another British feint, and refused to see it was the real thing.

Montcalm grimly marched for the Plains of Abraham with what men he could muster—about 5,000, the same size force as Wolfe's. There was no time to be spent trying to convince Vaudreuil and Ramesay of the danger, and no time to wait for the French forces to the west to come to Quebec's defense.

Montcalm was forced to take to the offensive for the first time. It was either that or surrender, or else starve. Quebec had only two days' food supply. If Montcalm took a defensive attitude, Wolfe would simply starve the city to defeat, or perhaps move his heavy cannon into position and knock down the already weakened walls.

It was about six in the morning when the French troops reached the Plains of Abraham. A light shower was falling. Montcalm sent out a forward party of sharpshooting militiamen and Indians to take cover in the bushes that dotted the broad plateau. Behind these skirmishers he arrayed his infantry. Wolfe's troops were already in position, in a two-deep battle line curving across the Plains from the cliffside.

At nine, Montcalm began the advance. His front line of sharpshooters did some damage, and among the victims was Wolfe, who was hit in the wrist. He casually wrapped his handkerchief around the wound, told his men to lie down, and sent sharpshooters of his own forward to skirmish.

The French continued to advance, cutting the distance between the lines from 600 yards to 200. The English remained silent, waiting. "Wait till they get near us," Wolfe ordered. "Then fire with a good aim."

Firing as they went, the French came forward. But their line became disorganized, because they had to throw themselves constantly to the ground to reload. Soon they formed an uneven, ragged line, some men standing and firing, others on the ground reloading. The British coolly held their fire. When the French were 130 yards away, the British troops rose from the ground for the first time. Wolfe's officers kept tight control, and every man obeyed. "Don't fire until they're close to us," they were told.

On the French came, firing steadily at the British. When only 100 yards separated the two lines, the British finally advanced, moving in unison toward the French rifles. Still they held their fire. Finally, when the French were but 40 yards away, the British rifles spoke. A volley rang out, sounding to the French "like a cannon shot."

A British historian, J. W. Fortescue, wrote, "With one deafening crash, the most perfect volley ever fired on battlefield burst forth as if from a single monstrous weapon, from end to end of the British line."

A cloud of smoke obscured the field. While it drifted upward, the British reloaded, and again fired as one man, stepping smartly forward four paces. Again they reloaded, again they advanced, again they fired.

The French were helpless before the methodical perfection of the British advance. After ten minutes the French were in full flight. But as they fled, a retreating soldier took aim at Wolfe. A shot passed through the young general, and a second one a moment later. Wolfe staggered and cried out, "Support me, support me, lest my gallant fellows should see me fall."

He was carried to the rear, but refused a surgeon. "It is needless," he murmured. "It is all over with me."

Then a cry went up: "They run, see how they run!"

"Who runs?" Wolfe asked faintly.

"The enemy, sir! They give way everywhere!"

Wolfe roused himself and gave his last orders—to cut off the flight of the fugitives. Then, falling back, he turned on his side, muttered, "Now God be praised, I will die in peace," and gave up his life.

Montcalm too was a casualty. He was wounded in the retreat and entered the gates of Quebec with blood streaming from his body. "It is nothing, it is nothing," he insisted, when the fear-stricken townspeople saw him ride in. But he died that evening.

The French armies were destroyed, and by 9 P.M. were in full retreat up the St. Lawrence. The British surrounded the town, and, though it held out futilely for a few more days, it finally surrendered on September 17. The Battle of the Plains of Abraham had broken the French strength; only 58 British soldiers had died, 562 had been wounded, while the French casualties numbered in the thousands.

The war did not end immediately, but the end was inevitable. As Fletcher Pratt put it in his account of the struggle, "Though the decapitated snake writhed for a while, the French dominion of Canada was ended." The following September, Amherst took Montreal, and the Treaty of Paris, signed in February 1763, gave all of Canada to the British, and most of India also, for the war had been carried on in Asia as well.

The results were far-reaching. At one stroke France lost the richest part of her overseas empire, and came upon hard times financially—setting in motion the chain of events that would lead, a generation later, to the French Revolution. At the same time Great Britain gained vast territories which would swell her wealth and make her the dominant nation of the world for the next century and a half. And England's American colonies, soon to win their independence, were freed forever from the threat of French domination.

And if the sentry had not let Wolfe's boats pass in the darkness? If the British had been cut to pieces as they tried to come ashore? Then all of Canada, and not merely the Province of Quebec, would speak French today, and probably New York and New England and Ohio as well. France herself might still be a kingdom today.

But these conjectures must remain in the world of if. France lost; Canada fell to England; an English-speaking republic eventually emerged along the Atlantic Coast. The future course of history for France, Great Britain, and the unborn United States of America was shaped in those 15 fierce minutes on the Plains of Abraham.

THE BATTLE OF VALCOUR ISLAND
A Revolution is Saved

C AN a battle which came to no real conclusion be called "decisive" in any way? And can this same inconclusive battle, which is so obscure few have ever heard of it, really be considered one of the decisive battles of world history?

I think so. I think the Battle of Valcour Island rates the title of "decisive," and full rank in the roll of history's turning points. If that battle had gone any other way, the American Revolution would have ended in 1776. The Union Jack would probably fly over the cities of North America today, and "God Save the Queen" would be our anthem.

The Battle of Saratoga, in 1777, is generally considered the decisive battle of the Revolutionary War. The two classic works on great battles, Creasy's *Fifteen Decisive Battles* and Fuller's *Military History of the Western World*, both list Saratoga as crucial to the colonists' cause.

141

But if a certain American general had not shown great bravery at Valcour Island the year before, there would have been no victory at Saratoga, and most likely no United States of America. The little-known battle is the keystone of the colonists' victory over England. It deserves to be more widely known.

The revolution had not been going well. The ragged, poorly armed colonists had little in their favor but pluck, determination, and the advantage of fighting on home soil. Their opponents were Europe's greatest military machine. The war had been going on since 1775, when British troops first engaged the rebels at Lexington and Concord. One of the outstanding American leaders was a young officer named Arnold, in his mid-thirties, a handsome, athletic man whose boldness and valor were extraordinary. In 1775, Colonel Arnold, Ethan Allen and the Green Mountain Boys took the British garrison at Fort Ticonderoga with ease, and then Arnold continued on to take the other British forts along Lake Champlain.

While American troops besieged Boston, Arnold was carrying the war into Canada. He believed that the Canadian settlers would join the men of the Thirteen Colonies in the uprising against Great Britain. In September 1775, Arnold entered Maine, and pushed across the St. Lawrence by December, joining forces with General Richard Montgomery, who had taken Montreal in November.

In a savage snowstorm the troops of Montgomery and Arnold advanced on Quebec on December 21. But the attack failed. Montgomery was killed, Arnold was badly wounded in the leg, and the invading force was nearly wiped out. The British had intercepted one of Arnold's messengers and had known in advance of the planned attack.

Arnold drew his decimated army back behind snow embankments and sent for reinforcements. But no reinforcements were to be had. The early rebel victories had given way to defeats. The Thirteen Colonies were still divided; many colonists opposed the revolution, and raising troops was a difficult chore for the Continental Congress and the revolution's newly chosen commander-in-chief, George Washington. Colonel Arnold continued to besiege Quebec through the spring of 1776, with his shadow of an army, until on April 2 he turned over command to another officer and withdrew to Montreal to recuperate from injuries sustained when thrown from his horse. The siege was lifted five weeks later when word came that British reinforcements had entered the mouth of the St. Lawrence.

The Canadian expedition had ended in disaster. The colonists retreated to Trois Rivières, midway between Montreal and Quebec, and attempted to capture that city, intending to use it as a jumping-off point for a second attack on Quebec. But they were driven off with heavy losses. Hundreds of Americans were captured, hundreds more were killed or lost in the swamps. There were only a dozen British casualties.

Licking their wounds, the Americans abandoned all hope of taking Canada. "Let us quit [Canada] and secure our own country before it is too late," Arnold wrote one of the other generals, pointing out wisely that there was "more honor in making a safe retreat than in hazarding a battle against such superiority." Eight thousand men, 2,000 of them suffering from smallpox and 1,500 victims of malaria or dysentery, crept back to Crown Point, on Lake Champlain, the place where the ill-fated Canadian expedition had started from in the fall of 1775, ten months before.

"Our Army at Crown Point," John Adams wrote, "is an object of wretchedness to fill a humane mind with horror; disgraced, defeated, discontented, diseased, naked, undisciplined, eaten up with vermin; no clothes, beds, blankets, no medicines; no victuals, but salt pork and flour."

The Continental Congress learned of the Trois Rivières defeat on June 17, and sent an experienced general, Horatio Gates, to take command of the American forces in Canada. But at that point there were no American forces in Canada. Gates went instead to Crown Point, where General Philip Schuyler held command over the remnants of the Canadian expedition and, after some dispute, Gates accepted second rank to Schuyler. The two generals, Colonel Arnold, and other officers conferred on July 5, the day of Gates' arrival, and the day after the Continental Congress, in Philadelphia, had signed the Declaration of Independence making the war official.

At Gates' suggestion the army abandoned Crown Point and retreated even farther to the south, to Ticonderoga, while sending the sick men still farther behind the lines. At Ticonderoga the Americans began to regroup their battered forces in August. Militiamen from New England gradually joined the army at Ticonderoga, and by August there were nearly 5,000 men fit for duty.

To the north, the British army was under the command of Sir Guy Carleton, the capable general who had driven off Arnold at Quebec the year before. Now Carleton was massing forces for a drive down Lake Champlain, the northern gateway to the colonies. If the British gained possession of Lake Champlain, they would have easy access to the Hudson River, and it would be simple for them to go on to capture Albany and then all of New England.

Colonel Arnold knew that Carleton was planning to move on the lake. Carleton was building boats at the north end of the lake. "We must have a fleet ready to block him," Arnold insisted. "Give me money to build ships!"

Arnold began with four ships, three of them captured from the British in previous encounters, the other one built at

Ticonderoga. These were the schooners *Royal Savage, Liberty,* and *Revenge,* and the sloop *Enterprise.* These four comprised what General Gates lightheartedly called "the American Navy." More ships had to be built, and quickly.

But Fort Ticonderoga was not equipped for building a navy from scratch. There were no tools, no sawmills, no skilled craftsmen. Ticonderoga was in the middle of a wilderness. Arnold's men were soldiers, not sailors. They hardly knew how to rig a ship, let alone how to build one.

Arnold persevered. He had 2,000 axes sent to him from Albany and Connecticut. Nails and tar and spikes, and canvas for sailcloth, were brought in from New England and Pennsylvania. Experienced carpenters and sailmakers came, too, though not out of patriotism; Arnold offered them the fantastically high wage of five dollars a day to come and build boats for him in the woods.

A fleet began to take shape in the wilderness.

Scouts kept Arnold posted on Carleton's doings, up in the north. Arnold learned that the British general had swelled his force from its original 8,000 to more than 13,000 with the addition of 5,000 German mercenaries. And Carleton had put together a powerful fleet. He had had ships taken apart and carried in pieces past the rapids to the lake, where they were reassembled. There was the *Inflexible,* a giant three-master armed with eighteen 12-pound cannon; the *Maria,* with fourteen 6-pounders; the *Carleton,* with a dozen more 6-pounders; the *Loyal Convert,* with seven 9-pounders; twenty smaller gunboats; and the pride of the flotilla, a huge flat-bottomed boat, almost a raft, the *Thunderer,* manned by 300 men and armed with six 24-pounders, six 12-pounders, and two howitzers.

Faced with a floating fortress of this magnitude, and two dozen other powerful ships, Arnold knew he could not hope

to compete in size. Instead he ordered small, highly maneu-
verable ships to be built: light, fast vessels that could outrun
and outsail Carelton's big boats.

Arnold had two kinds of boats built: row galleys and
gondolas. The row galleys, 70 to 80 feet long, were two-
masted ships with round bottoms. They looked more like
Mediterranean schooners than anything ever before seen in
North American waters, but they had the advantage of being
fast-moving and easy to handle by unskilled oarsmen like
Arnold's troops. Each row galley was equipped with eight to
ten guns—a 12-pounder and an 18-pounder in the bow, a pair
of 9-pounders in the stern, and four to six 6-pounders in
broadside. They were manned by 80 men each.

The gondolas were clumsy, flat-bottomed boats, 45 feet
long, with one mast. They were awkward things that could sail
only before the wind, but they were easy to build and were
fitted to carry 45 men and three guns, one 12-pounder and
two 9-pounders. Arnold was counting on his row galleys for
fast action, with the gondolas providing extra firepower.

By August 20, Arnold had six gondolas ready, along with
his four original ships and a fifth, the *Lee*, that had lately
joined his little fleet. While the row galleys were under construction, Arnold set about teaching his men some elementary
seamanship. On August 24, he put to sail from Crown Point
with his 11 vessels, and for the next month cruised Lake
Champlain, drilling his men in gunnery, tactics, and seamanship, and searching out possible sites for the battle to come.

Early in September, Arnold found his spot—Valcour
Island, about ten miles south of the Canadian border. It struck
him as "an exceeding fine and secure harbor," and on September 23 he dropped anchor there to await Carleton's arrival.

Valcour Island was about two miles long, slightly less than
a mile wide. Heavily wooded, it rose in some places 200 feet
above the level of the lake. Along the western side of the

island lay a narrow, shallow channel, too treacherous for ships of Carleton's fleet's size to use. Carleton would have to come down the eastern side of Valcour Island. Arnold saw that he could lie in wait, unseen, while the British fleet passed. A promontory would render his ships invisible to anyone coming down out of the north. And then, once Carleton's fleet had passed, Arnold could bring his little navy out of hiding and fall upon the British. The prevailing winds were northerly, so that the British, attacked unexpectedly from the rear, would be forced to turn and come upwind to defend themselves.

All during September, Arnold sent word to the main army under General Gates for 200 skilled sailors. His fleet, Arnold said, was made up of landlubbers, "very indifferent men in general." He told Gates, "Great part of those who shipped for seamen know very little of the matter. We have a wretched, motley crew in the fleet." He also wanted experienced gunners, and heavy clothing against the cold nights of October.

Arnold got nothing. He continued to ask right up until the day before the battle, without result. He would simply have to make do with his "wretched, motley crew."

More ships were leaving the boatyard, though. Two more gondolas, the *Jersey* and *Success*, joined the fleet at Valcour Island, and three row galleys, the *Washington, Trumbull,* and *Congress,* swelled the number of ships. He chose the *Congress* for his flagship. A fourth row galley, the *Gates,* was still under construction when the battle began.

Carleton sailed on October 4, with a fleet of five large ships and two dozen smaller ones. Arnold's homemade navy, waiting hidden at Valcour Island, consisted of 16 vessels in all, with about half the firepower of Carleton's fleet.

The British sailed cautiously southward along Lake Champlain. Scouts going ahead could find no sign of an American fleet. On October 10th, Carleton got word that American ships had been seen in the Valcour Island vicinity. But the ships were nowhere to be found. Canadian and Indian scouts patrolled the shore ahead of the fleet and had nothing to report.

On October 11, a gray, bleak day with a strong north wind blowing, the British fleet sailed past Valcour Island. For some reason, Carleton had not bothered to send out scouts that morning. Nor could his lookouts, high in the masts, see Arnold's 16 ships hidden in the cove. Serenely down the broad main channel of the lake the British sailed, passing the eastern shore of Valcour Island. Not till they were more than a mile south of the island did the British suspect they had been fooled. A British seaman looked back and gasped in shock. Five of Arnold's ships were coming round the southern tip of Valcour Island into open water!

Arnold had seen the tips of Carleton's masts at dawn, and his fleet was ready. There was little hope that his improvised navy could actually defeat Carleton's vastly superior fleet, but Arnold was not necessarily interested in victory. Delay was enough. Carleton had to be held back. Sir William Howe had just defeated General Washington in the Battle of Long Island, and the Revolutionary Army was badly off balance. If Carleton got through from Canada and cut southward across New York, the war would be over. It was as simple as that. Carleton had to be delayed.

The *Congress,* the *Royal Savage,* and three of the row galleys ventured from hiding first. Carleton's ships swung around immediately and began to beat their way upwind to give battle. When Arnold saw the British fleet coming at him in tight formation, he hurriedly gave orders for a retreat.

"Back to the cove," went the word from ship to ship.

The big British ships were having their difficulties, though. The giant *Thunderer* wallowed in the choppy water, making no headway against the wind. The *Inflexible* and the *Maria,* two of Carleton's biggest vessels, were unable to get within close range, and dropped anchor, relying on long-range bombardment instead. Only Carleton's small gunboats succeeded in drawing near the American fleet.

Arnold was managing the retreat in good order, matching the British fire as he drew back. The row galleys were performing well; they simply dropped sail and went back by oars against the wind. But the *Royal Savage*, Arnold's best and biggest ship, ran into trouble. She had no oars, and was having problems with the wind. As she rolled precariously, a British cannonball chopped her mainmast in two, and shot ripped her sails. Crippled—and badly handled by her captain, Arnold claimed—she swung around, ran into shore and grounded. The crew attempted to continue the fight from shore, but the ship's big guns pointed uselessly skyward and, under heavy pounding from the guns of the *Carleton*, they had to abandon the ship. Later in the day, boats from the *Carleton* and the *Thunderer* attempted to board her, but were driven back by American shells, and still later a crew from the *Maria* succeeded in boarding her and blowing the ship up.

The rest of Arnold's ships made it safely back to the cove. For several hours there was no action. Arnold arrayed his ships in a crescent at the mouth of the cove, and Carleton, unable to get upwind enough to mount a close-range attack, opened a long-range cannonade. Then, about noon, the schooner *Carleton* was caught by a shift in the wind and was carried within 350 yards of the American line. There it dropped anchor and began a close-quarter barrage.

The American ships closed in. Arnold himself manned the guns on the *Congress*. The *Carleton* was sorely pounded and all her officers were wounded or killed; a nineteen-year-old midshipman had to take command. For hours, the *Carleton* was mauled by American guns. By the time Carleton realized the ship was trapped, two feet of water were in her hold. Carleton sent two gunboats to the ship's aid, and then the mighty *Inflexible* entered the cove. It was nearly evening, now.

At point-blank range, the *Inflexible* boomed five broadsides into the American ships, working terrific damage. The American guns were silenced by the ferocity of the big ship's assault.

If the *Inflexible* had come into play earlier, it might have disabled the whole American fleet by itself. But as it was, night was swiftly falling, and a fog was closing in. The cautious Carleton drew the *Inflexible* back to a distance of 700 yards from the Americans, and the whole British fleet dropped anchor and continued firing until darkness descended. Then the British withdrew. Carleton knew just how tricky Arnold could be, and had no intention of remaining close to the Americans at night. In the morning, Carleton decided, the *Inflexible* would return and finish off Arnold's fleet in short order.

Aboard the *Congress* that night, the Americans took stock. They had fared poorly. Sixty men had been killed or wounded; three-fourths of their ammunition was gone. The *Congress* had been hulled a dozen times; the *Washington* had taken a shot through her mainmast; the *Royal Savage* had been destroyed; the *Philadelphia* had been so badly damaged that it had foundered an hour after the battle. It was impossible to face battle again the next day.

"We'll have to surrender," the discouraged Americans decided.

"No," Arnold said. "We'll slip out of the cove under cover of the fog."

The fog was so thick now that nothing could be seen more than 50 feet away. Arnold spurred his tired men to new exertion. Hooded lanterns were tied to the stern of each vessel, casting a light only backward. At seven that night, the row galley *Trumbull* slipped quietly out of the cove, the others following in single file, with the *Washington* and the *Congress* bringing up the rear.

They made it. They slipped through a gap in Carleton's line under cover of the blanket of fog. When they were out of earshot, the oars were broken out, and the crews hove to all through the night as the battered fleet crept away.

Dawn broke to reveal an empty cove. Carleton sputtered with rage and bewilderment.

"Follow them!" he roared. "Quickly! After them!"

The British left quickly indeed—so quickly that Carleton forgot to give his land forces any orders. When he realized this, after he had gone nearly eight miles, he had to turn back to inform his land troops of his plans.

The delay was all-important to the fleeing Americans. The *Trumbull,* the *Revenge,* the *Enterprise,* the *Lee,* and five of the gondolas were making good time, but the other five ships were laboring, and had to put in at Schuyler's Island, only eight miles south of Valcour. There it was decided that two of the gondolas, the *New York* and *Providence,* were too badly damaged to continue. Their equipment was removed and they were scuttled. A third gondola, the *Jersey,* ran aground and had to be abandoned. The *Congress* and the *Washington* set out together in early afternoon, hoping to catch up to the nine ships that had gone ahead.

But now the wind unexpectedly turned southerly. Arnold's two battered galleys made little progress. His men rowed doggedly for 16 hours and covered only six miles. And now the British fleet, moving steadily onward, was coming into sight, the *Maria* in the lead, the *Inflexible* and the *Carleton* just behind. At noon on October 13, they caught the *Congress,* the *Washington,* and three of Arnold's gondolas at Split Rock.

Arnold opened fire. The *Washington* was overwhelmed and quickly surrendered. The *Lee* ran ashore. Three British ships converged on the *Congress* and shot her sails to shreds, but Arnold refused to surrender. Of his crew of 73, only 46 still survived, but they fought on, until the capricious wind changed again. Arnold signaled, and his remaining ships headed for the east shore. The British, unable to follow, kept up a cannonade from the distance.

The American ships straggled to shore at Buttonmould Bay. Arnold ordered the ships put to the torch, and the men watched on the beach as the gallant vessels blazed. Then Arnold led his force inland, on the ten-mile trek to Crown Point. They arrived after darkness, escaping an Indian ambush on the way, and found the remnants of the fleet already there —the *Trumbull,* the *Enterprise,* the *Revenge,* the *Liberty,* and one of the gondolas.

The Battle of Valcour Island had ended in utter defeat for the fledgling American navy. Eleven of Arnold's 16 ships had been destroyed, and close to a 100 men killed and wounded. How could such a rout be called a decisive battle of the war?

Valcour Island was decisive because it created delay. Carleton could easily have come down Lake Champlain in August, and he would have met with no opposition. Instead, confused by word of Arnold's plans, Carleton waited until October, when he had assembled a powerful armada—much too powerful, considering the real nature of Arnold's fleet.

Arnold had won two months of time, and had caused a few more days of delay during the actual battle. By the time Carleton finally did get down Lake Champlain, it was mid-October and too late to accomplish anything. His next objective would have been Fort Ticonderoga, but Ticonderoga was strong enough to have held out until winter. So, having made his way as far as Crown Point, Carleton turned around and returned to Canada, having accomplished nothing all summer.

The Americans were busy, in the meanwhile. During the months of fall and winter, they were rebuilding their armies, strengthening their forts. By the time the British finally did come down, the Americans were able to resist them, and the course of events led to the great American victory at Saratoga that virtually settled the outcome of the war.

If Arnold had not befuddled and delayed Carleton, and if Carleton had sailed in August or September, Fort Ticonderoga would have fallen by October, and the English could have remained there through the winter, going on down the Hudson in spring and bringing the Revolution to a swift conclusion. So Valcour Island, though on the surface it seems to be a defeat, was actually a kind of victory, for it won precious time for the colonists.

And the hero of Valcour Island, Arnold? He had been named a brigadier general after his 1775 campaign in Canada and, after a brilliant victory at Ridgefield in April 1777, he was promoted to major general, and then to a full general after his valiant service in the two battles of Saratoga. But later in the war he quarreled with the other American leaders, became embittered, and turned against the Revolution. He attempted to betray the Americans to the British in 1780.

And so it is that the Battle of Valcour Island has failed to get its due in history. For it is hard to accept the ironic fact that the military genius who saved the Revolution through his courage and energy at Valcour Island was Benedict Arnold, whose name today is a synonym for traitor.

CHAPTER

THIRTEEN

THE BATTLE OF WATERLOO

The End of Napoleon's Dream

WHILE the new United States of America was strug-
gling with the problems of its infancy and childhood,
a bantam-sized ex-corporal from Corsica was reshaping the
course of European history. He was Napoleon Bonaparte,
born in 1769, who made himself master of France by the time
he was thirty, and then set out to conquer the world.

Napoleon entered the stream of history at a strategic time.
France had put her king to death and had destroyed her
aristocracy. A power vacuum existed, and Napoleon took
advantage of it. Attracting attention by his brilliant military
triumphs in Italy, he survived a disastrous campaign in Egypt
and came back to France, overthrew the five "Directors" who
had been governing the French Republic, and became one of
three "Consuls" that ruled France. Before very long Napoleon
held the rank of First Consul, for a term of ten years. By 1802,

he had been voted Consul for life, with the right to choose his successor. France was gradually creeping back to the system of hereditary monarchy that had been overthrown only a decade before.

In 1804 Napoleon carried his climb a step further. He arranged to be named Emperor of the French—the word "king" was looked on unfavorably since the revolution—and put the crown on his head with his own hands. With France his, Napoleon looked now to Europe.

The natural enemy of France was England. The two nations had been rivals in Europe for hundreds of years. Napoleon had tasted England's military power in Egypt, in 1798, when the British fleet under Lord Nelson destroyed the French fleet in the Battle of the Nile. In 1805 the same Nelson dealt Napoleon an even more crushing defeat at Trafalgar, again wrecking his fleet and putting permanent end to the possibility that Napoleon would ever successfully invade England.

Elsewhere in Europe Napoleon was more successful. He put his own brother on the throne of Spain, annexed Holland and made another brother king there, conquered much of Germany, Austria, and Italy. 1810 saw him master of most of Continental Europe. But then the tide turned against him.

One major turning point was the Russian campaign of 1812. Napoleon marched deep into Russia and burned Moscow—but, as we will see later on, it is often easier to lead an invading army into Russia than to get it out safely again. The disastrous French retreat from Moscow saw Napoleon's army slaughtered, and soon all Europe was in revolt against him. Spain, Holland, Belgium, Prussia, Austria all rose and threw off the shackles of France. Napoleon's gaudy empire, which had once embraced three quarters of Europe, collapsed overnight. Allied armies under Lord Wellington drove him back to France, and on April 11, 1814, with his empire dwindling by the hour, Napoleon abdicated the throne. The French monarchy was restored and fat King Louis XVIII came to Paris to rule.

Napoleon was given an island to rule—the island of Elba, a dot of land in the Mediterranean between Italy and Napoleon's native island of Corsica. A British frigate escorted the ex-emperor to his island of exile in late April 1814, and all Europe hoped that the troublesome Napoleon would not be heard from again.

Napoleon had other ideas.

He languished on Elba for almost a year, while the allied nations who defeated him dictated peace terms to France that sheared her of all territory acquired after 1792. But the allies quarreled among themselves as they debated the carving-up of Napoleon's empire. The Czar of Russia demanded all of Poland, and seemed willing to go to war to get it. England, France, and Austria formed a new alliance to deal with the Russian threat. In France, the restored King Louis was unpopular, and the people, remembering the glories of the Napoleonic decade, talked of a second revolution to drive the fat king from his throne.

Napoleon, on Elba, heard reports of all this: dissension between the allies, grumbling against King Louis in France. Only forty-five, restless on Elba and eager to return to power, Napoleon decided on a bold venture: to escape from the little island and stake his claim once again to sovereignty.

It was a foolhardy idea. In 1814 his own people had forced him to give up his throne for the good of France. Why did he think they would welcome him back now? Only a Napoleon would have made the attempt.

His captors were so confident that he would remain on Elba that they had even allowed him to maintain a small army of loyal troops, and a few ships. The guard placed around the island was a skimpy one. On February 26, 1815, Napoleon and 1,050 of his men slipped through the French guard in seven small ships, and on March 1 he landed in the Bay of St. Juan, on the Mediterranean. He set out to march northward across the French Alps toward Paris.

It was a triumphant march. From town to town spread the word that the emperor had returned, and the French turned out to cheer him. On March 7, he reached Grenoble, where he was confronted by a regiment loyal to King Louis. An officer spied him and called out, "There he is! Fire on him!"

Napoleon glanced at Colonel Mallet, who commanded his bodyguard, and said coolly, "Order the soldiers to put their muskets under their left arms, muzzles down." Then he stepped forward and declared, "Soldiers of the Fifth Regiment, do you know me? Here is your emperor. Who will may shoot."

A cry of "Long live the emperor!" burst from every throat. Napoleon continued his triumphant advance. By this time word had reached the allies—still meeting at Vienna to dispose of Napoleon's empire—that Napoleon had escaped and would have to be defeated all over again.

France welcomed him joyously. King Louis XVIII, quickly sensing which way the wind blew and remembering what had happened to the last French king to be overthrown, hurriedly slipped out of the country. On March 20 Napoleon reached Paris and was hailed as emperor.

Master politician that he was, Napoleon appealed to the broad mass of the people. Louis XVIII had favored the nobles and priests; Napoleon told the people, "I come to free you from bondage and serfdom," and authorized new, liberal laws for the benefit of the common folk, who had always liked him since he had risen from their own rank.

Now began the period known as the Hundred Days. Napoleon knew he must move swiftly. The allies could not tolerate his return, and would have to send new armies against him. Therefore, he had to raise troops of his own, be prepared to defend the borders of France, and make his position as emperor firm again immediately. Then, and only then, could he set out once again to conquer Europe. That dream had never died in him.

The four quarreling allies—Russia, England, Austria, and Prussia—quickly patched up their differences and set about mobilizing an army of 600,000 to trounce Napoleon. The emperor, for his part, started with an army of 150,000, but by June 1 had more than doubled it.

The main body of Allied troops was stationed in Belgium. These were British, Dutch and Prussian troops under command of two formidable generals—the Duke of Wellington and the Prussian Marshal Blücher. They had 220,000 troops under their command. On the upper Rhine, an Austrian army of 210,000 men under Prince Schwartzenberg was camped; 150,000 Russian soldiers under Barclay de Tolly were on the Middle Rhine; and an Austro-Italian army numbering about 75,000 was in northern Italy.

The plan was to demolish Napoleon's army by sheer weight of manpower. Wellington, Blücher, and Schwartzenberg were to march toward Paris, with Frimont attacking Lyons at the same time, and Barclay holding his army in reserve to come to the aid of the others when needed.

Napoleon boldly resolved to seize the initiative. He saw that if he struck first, he might prevent this vast Allied army from closing in on him. The Allies were spread out over half of Europe, and could not meet to attack him before July 1. A sudden thrust into Belgium, Napoleon reasoned, might defeat the armies of Wellington and Blücher, and then he could turn to deal with the Austrians and Russians afterward. His gamble was that if he defeated the Allies in Belgium, he would get support from other nations in Europe.

Early in June, Napoleon began to gather his forces for the assault. He was risking everything on one stunning victory that would lay his enemies in confusion.

A triple chain of fortresses protected France on her border with Belgium. Behind this screen Napoleon assembled his troops. On June 13, 1815, the French army reached Avesnes, where Napoleon was joined by the veteran Marshal Ney.

The Allied troops were strung out across Belgium for some 90 miles. Napoleon chose to strike at the very center, at Charleroi. The Allies were aware that this was his probable strategy, and they had laid plans to counter it. When Napoleon moved toward Charleroi, the two Allied flanks would descend on him from right and left and swamp him with their numerical superiority.

But the Allies did not expect Napoleon to move his army into position so swiftly or so silently. French troops, 124,000, were massed for the attack on Charleroi by June 14, and the Allies suspected nothing. On that day Napoleon posted a stirring "Order of the Day," in which he told his troops, "To every Frenchman who has a heart, the moment is now arrived to conquer or to die!"

And by dawn the French army was on the march toward Charleroi.

The Allies, caught by surprise, could offer little resistance, and by noon on the 15th, Napoleon had taken Charleroi. Marshal Blücher, finally realizing what was happening, was slowly concentrating his own troops not far away, at Sombreffe. Wellington, far to the north in Brussels, was unsure of the course of Napoleon's plans, and for the moment held back, leaving Blücher in an exposed position. By nightfall on the 15th, thanks to Allied confusion, Napoleon was in an excellent strategical position. His army was concentrated in a square 12 miles on a side, and had cut off Wellington's army from Blücher's, so that Napoleon could move with equal ease against either army.

The morning of the 16th saw Napoleon proceeding with confidence. His army was divided into two wings and a reserve. He planned to bring the reserve into action to aid whichever of the two wings seemed to be leading the attack, while the other wing would be used purely to hold the enemy at bay and neutralize enemy troops.

Napoleon gave Marshal Ney command of the left wing and sent him to take the town of Quatre Bras, to the west. The emperor planned to move the right wing and the reserve forward to attack Blücher, just to the northeast. Having defeated Blücher while Ney was preventing attack in the west, Napoleon would then swing westward, join with Ney, and march northward on Brussels to deal with Wellington. In that way Napoleon would not have to face the combined might of both Allied armies. Dealing with them one at a time, he stood a chance of victory.

While these plans were being hatched, Wellington was slowly coming to realize the seriousness of the situation. At first he could not believe Napoleon was actually taking the offensive. But on June 15th, hearing that Napoleon had captured Charleroi, Wellington came to see what was happening. "Napoleon has humbugged me!" he burst out angrily. "He has gained twenty-four hours' march on me." And he hurriedly ordered his army to march for Quatre Bras.

Wellington and Napoleon, the two most celebrated generals of their day, had never faced each other in battle before. They were of the same age, and each had a dictatorial, autocratic frame of mind. But where Napoleon believed in striking out boldly, Wellington was more cautious. He preferred to let the enemy attack, and then to counterattack with grim effect. He was a master of defensive warfare and of the powerful counterattack.

As Wellington headed for Quatre Bras, 25 miles south of Brussels, Napoleon prepared to move against Blücher. Ney, at Quatre Bras, was moving with mysterious slowness. He let his chance to take the town easily slip by, and by the time he pressed the attack, Wellington's troops had already arrived. Napoleon, meanwhile, went into action against Blücher, thinking that if he encountered difficulties he could always recall Ney from Quatre Bras.

By 3:15 Napoleon realized that Blücher's Prussians were too strong for him. He sent word to Ney to march eastward and fall upon Blücher's right wing and rear. "The army in our front is lost if you act with energy," Napoleon wrote. "The fate of France is in your hands. Thus do not hesitate even for a moment to carry out the maneuver."

But Ney had waited too long to attack Quatre Bras, and instead of facing 7,500 Dutch troops, he had had to take on 20,000 of Wellington's best. Obviously Ney could not withdraw and come to Napoleon's aid. The best he could do was to detach one corps, under D'Erlon, to help the emperor. But then new troops joined Wellington, and now Ney could not even spare D'Erlon. He sent a messenger to order D'Erlon to return to Quatre Bras.

D'Erlon, who had already moved eastward, now swung his corps back toward Ney. Almost at once came another message from Napoleon: he needed reinforcements at once. Where was D'Erlon? Ney, by this time sorely pressed, refused to release D'Erlon, who was slowly marching back toward Quatre Bras.

Still more reinforcements reached Wellington, and by nightfall the French under Ney were severely beaten. D'Erlon's corps did not return until 9, and the battle was over by then. Seeing that nothing could be done at Quatre Bras, poor D'Erlon ordered another reverse, and started his men back to Ligny, where Napoleon was hard pressed by Blücher.

The emperor's forces held their own at Ligny, however, and by 7:45 the tide of battle changed in their favor. The center of Blücher's army gave way, and the Prussians retreated. As night fell, Blücher had been beaten—but not destroyed.

It could have been a day of major victory for the French.

But blunders had cost them success. Why had Ney not taken Quatre Bras in the morning, for instance? Then he would have been free to send troops to Napoleon's aid, and Blücher might have been routed instead of merely driven back. And D'Erlon's corps had wandered back and forth between the two battlefields all day without firing a single shot at either. The presence of D'Erlon at Quatre Bras would probably have beaten Wellington; if he had fought at Ligny, Blücher would have fallen. As it was, nothing had been accomplished.

Napoleon had made a blunder of his own. That morning he had left his reserves, under Lobau, at Charleroi, and he failed to order them forward until late in the day. Had he had these troops at Ligny, D'Erlon could have remained at Quatre Bras, and the French would probably have carried both battles.

Still, Napoleon had done well at Ligny. He had hurt Blücher badly. Now he had to turn on Wellington.

More confusion followed the next day, June 17. Communications between Napoleon's camp and Ney were poor, and Napoleon had only the vaguest idea of what was happening at Quatre Bras. Wellington, for his part, had not yet heard of Blücher's defeat at Ligny. On the morning of the 17th, learning of the result at Ligny, Wellington decided to withdraw from Quatre Bras. Now was the time for Ney to reopen hostilities and pin Wellington at Quatre Bras until Napoleon's army could arrive. But for the second day running, Ney took the course of inaction. He let Wellington slip away. When Napoleon arrived, only a few trailing detachments of Wellington's cavalry could be seen.

Napoleon was astonished to find that Ney had not taken the field against Wellington. Certain victory had been allowed to slip away. "France has been ruined," Napoleon told D'Erlon furiously. He gave orders for an immediate pursuit of Wellington.

A sudden thunderstorm came up, turning the sky black.

Rain descended in sheets, drenching the ground. The French were unable to advance through the mud, and Wellington made good his retreat. The outcome might have been entirely different had Napoleon been able to pursue.

June 18 saw the remnants of Blücher's forces pulling northward as well. Blücher and Wellington decided to retreat as far as Waterloo, a village south of Brussels, and there regroup and stand fast against Napoleon's advance. Wellington arrayed his troops at Waterloo while Blücher began to march north to meet him.

The field of Waterloo was two and a quarter miles deep, four miles wide, and that morning the ground was still soaked from the heavy rainfall. A highway cut the field in two. Low ridges ran across the field at north and south, with a shallow valley, about 45 feet deep, between them.

Wellington posted his main line on the northern ridge. He planned to stand fast and hold off Napoleon's army until Blücher could arrive and fall on the exposed right wing of the French. Napoleon arrayed his men, 74,000 strong, in three lines, some 1,300 yards from Wellington's position, along the southern ridge.

Napoleon chose to try to break Wellington's center. It is thought by many experts that this was a critical mistake, that the emperor would have done better to attack Wellington's left and prevent Blücher's army from joining his. But Napoleon was not expecting Blücher. The emperor had sent a detachment under General Grouchy to keep Blücher away. What Napoleon did not know was that Grouchy, a man of slow wits, had totally misread his orders and was at that moment actually pushing Blücher *toward* Waterloo.

At half-past eleven Napoleon began the battle with an attack on Wellington's right wing. This was strictly a feint, and it gained little. An inconclusive bombarbment continued for more than an hour, while Napoleon massed the main body of his troops for a direct attack on the English center. Four columns of infantry, totaling 18,000 men, were supported by a strong cavalry division and 74 heavy guns. This force was to be led by Ney, in whose military reputation Napoleon still had faith despite his bungles of the 16th and 17th.

But Napoleon had erred in waiting so long to begin. He had held off till the ground had dried, so that he could move his heavy guns around easily. What he did not know was that Grouchy had bungled. Perhaps Napoleon could have defeated Wellington alone, had he attacked at ten or eleven in the morning. But now it was one—and now, out of the woods, Prussians advanced! Grouchy had somehow blundered, and Blücher was joining forces with Wellington!

The turn of events dismayed Napoleon. A lesser man might have pulled back to rethink his strategy, but the emperor was too deeply committed. He sent Ney against Wellington's center all the same. D'Erlon's corps succeeded in routing a Dutch-Belgian brigade, but Wellington's British troops held firm and drove the attackers back, with heavy loss on both sides.

Since the Prussians still had not entered the battle, Napoleon sent Ney to make a second attempt. A second time the attack failed. Then the Allied line drew back to gain more cover, and Ney pressed the attack, only to find his men entangled and being cut down. Again, Napoleon's generalship failed him. He sent cavalry in without supporting them with infantry. No doubt he was growing tired, and failing to think through his plans with his old genius.

Now the Prussians began to enter the conflict. Desperately, Napoleon ordered Ney to take the village of La Hay Sainte, the key of Wellington's position and, about 6, Ney finally succeeded, not without tremendous cost in men. Wellington's center was badly shaken. Wellington did his best to steady his troops. He moved whatever reinforcements he could find toward the center, bolstering it. More and more Prussians were arriving at the battlefield all the while. Napoleon sent his best men, the Old Guard, against Wellington, but failed to make a dent. About 8, the Old Guard was driven back, and suddenly the Prussians broke through the French line on the northeast. Two battalions of the Guard stood firm, but the rest of the French army turned in flight.

Wellington and Blücher now came together at 9:15, with victory in their grasp. Napoleon's troops had been unable to withstand the combined assault. The Allies gave chase, following the fleeing French all night. The French had lost 40,000 men and all their artillery; 7,000 Prussians and 15,000 of Wellington's men had perished, and the bodies lay thickly piled on the field of Waterloo.

Napoleon reached Paris on June 21 and found himself without friends. Word of his defeat had preceded him. Those who had hailed him at the beginning of the Hundred Days now turned against him. As in April 1814, he saw that he had lost all support. For the second time he abdicated, naming his infant son as emperor.

The forces of Blücher and Wellington cut through France with ease. On July 9, Louis XVIII returned to Paris. Napoleon had slipped into the countryside, planning to escape to the United States, but he fell into British hands and asked asylum in the land of his old enemies.

No one quite knew what to do with Napoleon. The British did not want the responsibility of putting him to death, but they hardly cared to have him setting up as a political refugee in London. So it was decided to confine him a second time to an island. The British did not make the mistake of sending him to Elba this time. They shipped him off to the remote Atlantic island of St. Helena, where he was kept under close guard for the remaining six years of his life. His dream of

European dominance was at its end. He died in his fifty-second year, and his gravestone simply reads HERE LIES—without even a name.

Waterloo was decisive because it could so easily have gone the other way. Napoleon was, perhaps, a sick man and a tired one, and certainly Marshal Ney and General Grouchy were incompetent soldiers. If Ney had taken Quatre Bras, if Grouchy had kept Blücher away from Waterloo, if Napoleon had not made so many ill-advised choices during those fatal four days—

If. If. Always if. Certainly victory was in Napoleon's grasp in June 1815, and he let it slip through. As a result, his dream of empire failed, and the victorious Allies were able to establish the political order that dominated Europe for the next hundred years. The downfall of France left England supreme on the seas, and also had the effect of setting in motion the forces that, later in the century, would create a powerful and unified Germany out of dozens of small states. Prussia emerged to take France's place as a major European power. Within two generations Prussia had become Germany, and the stage was set for the two titanic conflicts that would convulse Europe in the twentieth century.

And had Napoleon won at Waterloo? Then England and France would have grappled for the control of Europe all through the nineteenth century, and Germany would have remained disunited, or even subjugated to France.

But Napoleon lost. The little man with grandiose dreams ended his days a prisoner on St. Helena. He did not get a third chance.

CHAPTER

FOURTEEN

THE BATTLE OF GETTYSBURG
The Dashing of Confederate Hopes

THERE is no kind of war more bitter, more regrettable, than civil war. Brother's hand is raised against brother, and a divided nation writhes in agony.

From 1861 to 1865 the United States knew that agony. Although secession sparked the war, slavery was the issue: a disagreement between the states of the North and those of the South over whether human beings could be kept in bondage in the United States. The South insisted they could, and went to war to defend their privilege. The North denounced slavery, and fought to prevent the South from continuing it. The result was a savage war whose wounds are yet to heal, a century later. The South has never forgiven the North for interfering in its way of life, and resentment lies close to the surface.

All during the decade of the 1850s the quarrel raged. The North recognized it could not abolish slavery in the South,

167

but it was determined to prevent new states from entering the Union as slave states. While the slaveholding South slumbered in its genteel ways, the dynamic North was expanding westward. The states of the South soon saw that they were being forced into a minority position.

The presidential election of 1860 brought a new man of a new political party to the White House. The Republican, Abraham Lincoln, was elected entirely by the votes of the free states. The South forthwith decided to withdraw from the Union. On December 20, 1860, South Carolina seceded, followed swiftly by six other Southern states. By February, the seceders had set up the Confederate States of America, with Jefferson Davis as President.

The North did not recognize the right of these states to secede, and this is the ticklish legal problem that the South still debates. Why not let the South secede? Why insist on making war to drive slavery from the South? Why not let the Confederacy alone?

Lincoln did not see it that way. He felt that the North had a moral right to drive slavery from the United States, and that the secession was an illegal act. Civil war was the only alternative, and hostilities began in the spring of 1861.

The odds favored the powerful, industrial North over the weak, rural South. That the war lasted as long as it did is the result of the natural tendency of men to fight fiercely to defend their homeland and their way of life. Whatever one thinks of the institution of slavery—and I see no way of approving it—one has to admire the gallant battle the South waged. It fought nobly to defend its right to hold men in bondage, a splendid defense of a shabby cause.

Some Confederates knew that they had little hope of actually defeating the North. Their alternate goal was to wear the Union down, to fight an endless defensive war until the Northerners wearied of strife and recognized the secession.

But the early days of the war saw a series of colorful Confederate victories. As a result the South developed an exaggerated idea of its own strength, which led to rashness later on. And the North came to overrate the Confederate striking power, leading to overcaution and defensiveness.

The war seesawed along through 1861 and 1862. Gradually the two main military leaders came to the fore—dashing, aristocratic Robert E. Lee of the Confederacy, and whiskey-drinking, coarse Ulysses S. Grant of the North. Grant's rough-and-ready methods of warfare astonished his Union colleagues and left the Confederates bewildered. The Union general William Sherman, dazzled by a risky Grant maneuver that just happened to work, once remarked of him, "I am a better general than he is, but I lack his iron nerve."

But Grant, in 1862, was only one of many Union generals. The others were not all military geniuses. And so it happened that in the summer of 1862 Union troops approached the Confederate capital of Richmond, Virginia, and—with the power to capture it and end the war—somehow failed to take the city. Lee, at the same battle, also mysteriously failed to take advantage of an opportunity to smash the Union forces. The war might have been decided, one way or the other, in 1862, but for these two unaccountable lapses.

During the year that followed that fumbled battle, each side tried to gain the other's capital, and five major battles were fought: Bull Run, Antietam, Fredericksburg, Chancellorsville, and finally—on July 1–3, 1863—Gettysburg. In three of these five—Bull Run, Fredericksburg, and Chancellorsville— Lee bested the Union generals. Yet by the time the fifth had been fought, at Gettysburg, there was no longer any hope for the cause of secession, and the stage was set for Grant's victories at Vicksburg and Chattanooga, which broke the back of the Confederacy.

Gettysburg was something of an accident. Neither the

Union nor the Confederacy really planned to have a battle there, in southern Pennsylvania.

Lee was undertaking a desperate Confederate maneuver: a last ditch attempt to capture Washington, D. C. He thought, perhaps wrongly, that if Washington fell into Southern hands, the Union would panic and fall to defeat. Panic was the only hope of the Confederacy now, for the South had suffered heavy losses and was having difficulty remaining in its defensive position. On the principle that the best defense is a good offense, Lee marched northward on June 2, 1863. He had about 75,000 soldiers, and he was entering territory occupied by 175,000 Union troops.

His plan was to plunge deep into enemy territory and come down on the Union capital from the north, provisioning his army in a free state. Throughout June, Lee advanced into Pennsylvania, and the end of the month found him 100 miles north of Washington, on the Susquehanna River. His army was divided and scattered along a wide front. The Union army, which had been badly hurt at the Battle of Chancellorsville in May, was far to the south.

Lee had divided his army into three corps, commanded by Generals Longstreet, Ewell, and Hill. Hill's corps had the assignment of holding the Union troops in the south, under Hooker, while the rest of Lee's forces moved to the north. But by June 25, Hooker had shaken free of Hill and had crossed the Potomac in pursuit of Lee.

Lee had sent his cavalry, under Jeb Stuart, to Ewell's right. But Stuart made the mistake of taking the long way round, and Lee was thus deprived of his cavalry at a critical time. On June 28, Lee learned that Hooker had been replaced by the more capable General Meade, and that the Union army was coming after him.

Lee immediately ordered his scattered troops to concentrate in one area, at Cashtown, Pennsylvania. From there, he could menace both Washington and Baltimore, and also manage a retreat to the south if Meade proved troublesome.

Meade had a cavalry division in nearby Gettysburg. But there was no plan to fight a battle there. On June 30, a Confederate brigade of Hill's corps rode to Gettysburg for a fresh stock of shoes, and was surprised to find it held by Union cavalry. The next day, Hill brought up two divisions to cover the town. Lee's other two corps, under Ewell and Longstreet, were north of Gettysburg, and began to move on the town. And so, almost accidentally, the Battle of Gettysburg began.

The opening day's fighting took place first west of the town, then north, and finally northeast. The Union cavalry under Buford fought briskly; the Confederates, though they had not expected to fight, met fire with fire, and the first clash went to the Confederates. The outnumbered Union cavalry had to retreat through Gettysburg to Cemetery Hill, southeast of the town, and the two infantry corps that had gone to Buford's aid were cut to pieces.

But the Northerners dug in at Cemetery Hill. Lee, reaching the battlefield late in the day, told Ewell to take the hill "if practicable," but it proved not to be practicable, at least in Ewell's opinion. Later opinions hold that Ewell could probably have taken the hill and completed the rout.

During the night, reinforcements joined the Union troops, and Meade was able to regroup his men and prepare them for a full-scale battle the next day. The position looked encouraging for the Confederates, even so. If Meade were defeated, Lee would be able to march unopposed on Washington. If the battle went to the North, though, Lee still could retreat and try again at a later time.

The second day of fighting began with the Union troops securely dug in in the hills to the south of the town, holding a fishhook-shaped position with the shaft running north from steep, rocky hills called the Round Tops to Cemetery Hill, and the barb east of Cemetery Hill at Culp's Hill. By this time Meade's total army numbered 106,000, or about the size of Wellington and Blücher's combined force at Waterloo. Lee's army of 75,000 was roughly the size of Napoleon's. Neither the Northern army nor Lee's had had much battle experience.

The Confederates moved slowly in. An attack early on the morning of the 2nd might have caught the Northerners unprepared, but Lee and Longstreet did not fully grasp this, and it was not until four in the afternoon that Longstreet finally attacked, on the extreme Union left. The Confederates charged, letting rip the rebel yell that a Union chaplain called "an unearthly, fiendish yell, such as no other troops or civilized beings ever uttered."

The Confederate charge was fierce and the fighting heavy. For a while the Northerners were driven back. But Meade brought reinforcements up to steady the weakening center. And communications between the Southern generals were poor. While Longstreet was pressing the advance, Hill was falling back, and Ewell did not even get started until 6 o'clock. If the attack had been coordinated, the army of Meade would have been shattered that day.

If. Always *if.* Meade's men held Cemetery Hill. The Northern casualties were 9,000, and 7,000 Southern ones were registered, but the Union troops had not been dislodged.

Dawn of the third day brought a new Confederate strategy. Instead of attacking the rough ground at the Round Tops, Lee now intended to concentrate a double attack on Meade's right and center. Ewell would attack Meade on the extreme right, at Culp's Hill, and Longstreet would pound away in the center. Then, as Meade began to give ground under the assault, fresh Confederate troops led by General George E. Pickett would charge Meade's center and break through, followed by Hill's corps.

Ewell began the assault on Culp's Hill, but the Union men

fought back determinedly. After four hours of hard fighting the Confederates were driven off the hill entirely. But Lee decided to go ahead with the rest of this plan despite Ewell's defeat. Longstreet would attack Meade's center and soften it up for Pickett's charge.

Longstreet formed a line of 75 guns, with 65 guns of Hill's division to his left. The Union army had only 77 heavy guns of its own to reply with. All morning, the two armies faced each other, and finally, at one o'clock, Longstreet opened fire.

He shelled the Union position for an hour. Ammunition began to run low. The time was coming for Pickett's charge, and the worried Longstreet saw the disaster shaping up. The artillery of Hill and Ewell, on the left, was not effective, and his own guns were running low. Pickett's men would have to cross open fields without artillery support, charging a securely held Union post.

Why, then, did Pickett charge? It seems that only Longstreet knew the true suicidal nature of the situation, and Longstreet did not want to cancel the charge on his own authority. Lee, elsewhere on the field, had not known of the shortage of ammunition of Longstreet's artillery.

And Pickett charged.

The astonished Union men gaped as the Confederate brigades, almost entirely unsupported by heavy artillery, charged across the 1,200 yards of open country that separated the two lines. Then the defenders set up their heavy fire. On Pickett's men came, into a sheet of flame. They fell by hundreds as Union riflemen cut them down.

Amazingly, some of Pickett's men made it. Those on the left reached the Union position only to be driven back, but some of the men on the right miraculously broke into the Northern lines and did heavy damage. But the attack could not be sustained. Pickett's men fell back as Meade's troops closed ranks. They retreated under heavy fire. Of Pickett's

4,800 men, 3,393 were left lying on the field. The charge had been sheer madness.

As the shattered Confederate troops retreated, Lee came to meet them and encourage them. "It is I that have lost this fight, and you must help me out of it in the best way you can," he told them.

Meade's forces were too badly crippled to follow up their momentary advantage, and the belated arrival of the Confederate cavalry under Stuart kept them from attempting a major counterattack. The last battle of the day saw the Union duplicate Pickett's wild charge on a smaller scale. A brigade of Union cavalry launched a desperate charge, and was massacred. Then darkness fell.

The next day, Lee remained at Gettysburg in case Meade pressed the attack. But Meade did not, and on July 5 Lee began to retreat. He slipped away to the south. Meade unaccountably failed to follow up and cut Lee off. Lincoln was enraged when he heard that Meade had let Lee escape, and angrily declared, "There is bad faith somewhere."

Gettysburg, like Waterloo, was a battle in which an outnumbered army, given little chance of success, could easily have carried the day if only critical blunders had been avoided. Lee's subordinates at Gettysburg handled themselves poorly, and their poor coordination ruined the Confederate chance for victory. Indeed, only luck kept Lee from falling into Union hands at Gettysburg, which would have meant the end of the war right then and there.

Gettysburg is decisive because of its near-miss quality. Had Lee routed Meade on July 3, 1863, Washington might well have fallen into Confederate hands. That would have been the kind of symbolic triumph, unimportant strategically, which would have lifted Southern morale and perhaps demoralized the North to the extent that Lincoln would have asked for an armistice. In that case, the secession of the South would have been permanenly recognized, and the Confederate States of America would still be an independent slaveholding republic in the Western Hemisphere.

But Lee's generals failed him, and Meade held firm. The Confederates lost 30,000 irreplaceable men and were forced to slink back to Virginia with nothing gained. Never again in the war would they venture so far north, and never again would the outcome of the struggle be a matter for serious doubt. The Civil War had reached its turning point, and the tide had gone against the South. Soon Grant would triumph at Vicksburg, and then only a cleanup operation remained.

Four months after the battle, on November 19, 1863, President Lincoln journeyed to Gettysburg to dedicate the field as a national cemetery. Speaking of "the brave men, living and dead, who struggled here," Lincoln declared, the world "can never forget what they did here." And he urged his listeners to dedicate themselves "to the unfinished work which they who fought here have thus far so nobly advanced."

By April 1865, that unfinished work was completed when Lee surrendered to Grant at Appomattox, though an assassin's bullet robbed the President of his chance to heal the nation's great wounds. And so the bitterness born of the Civil War still plagues the United States after a hundred years. But the downfall of slavery was insured that day at Gettysburg when Union rifles cut Pickett's charging men to shreds.

CHAPTER
FIFTEEN

THE BATTLE OF STALINGRAD

Hitler's Crucial Mistake

THE year was 1941. All Europe was plunged into darkness and chaos. Goose-stepping conquerors from Germany, driven to a frenzy of murderous excitement by a new Napoleon who called himself Adolf Hitler, had marched unstoppably into a dozen nations. First Austria, then Czechoslovakia, Poland, the Netherlands, France, the Balkan countries—there was no stopping the Nazi legions. Greece fell. Yugoslavia fell. Only Great Britain, battered but determined, still held out against the Nazis by the summer of 1941, and it was only a matter of time before Britain would have to collapse under the repeated Nazi blows.

A new dark age was threatening the world. Germany and her two allies, Japan and Italy, were building an empire of tyranny that soon would cover most of the globe. And the two nations best able to resist the Axis Powers were not in the war.

The United States, still wrapped in isolation, was neutral, though actively supporting Britain's valiant struggle for survival. The Soviet Union, Europe's second mightiest power, was also on the sidelines. In August 1939, Russia and Nazi Germany had signed a ten-year mutual nonaggression pact. For the next two years, Russia stood aloof while Hitler's tanks rolled into country after country.

And then, on June 22, 1941, Hitler overreached himself. Practically to the day, 129 years after Napoleon had invaded Russia, Hitler deliberately broke his pact with the Soviet Union and ordered an invasion of that country.

It was to prove disastrous for the Nazi cause. Writing on the day of the invasion to his ally Mussolini, Hitler said, "The partnership with the Soviet Union, in spite of the complete sincerity of my efforts to bring about a final conciliation, was nevertheless often very irksome to me. . . . I am happy now to be delivered from this torment."

It was an insane miscalculation. On that day Hitler guaranteed his eventual defeat.

On the same day, British Prime Minister Winston Churchill went on the air to tell his people what had happened. Churchill said, "At four o'clock this morning Hitler attacked and invaded Russia. All his usual formalities of perfidy were observed with scrupulous technique. A nonaggression treaty had been solemnly signed and was in force between the two countries. No complaint had been made by Germany of its nonfulfillment. Under its cloak of false confidence the German armies grew up in immense strength along a line which stretched from the White Sea to the Black Sea. . . .

"Then suddenly, without declaration of war, without even an ultimatum, the German bombs rained down from the sky upon the Russian cities, German troops violated the Russian frontiers, and an hour later the German Ambassador, who during the night before was lavishing his assurances of friendship—almost of alliance—upon the Russians, called upon the Russian Foreign Minister to tell him that a state of war existed between Germany and Russia."

Hitler's Russian campaign began with a series of striking successes. By July 5, German troops were 450 miles inside Russia, and little more than 200 miles from Moscow. They turned on the Ukraine, capturing 600,000 Russians east of Kiev. The Germans used the same tactic again and again, encircling vast numbers of Russian soldiers and forcing them to surrender.

But somehow, no matter how many hundreds of thousands of Russians were captured, there were always more. Hitler's army was being drawn deeper and deeper into Russia. And then the advance began to lose steam. Hitler's generals quarreled, disagreeing over which part of the giant country to attack first. August passed, and September, without any important German victories. Time was running short. Hitler had hoped to defeat Russia entirely before the coming of winter, for he knew that no fighting could take place in the severe Russian cold.

In October 1941, the Germans again began to move. On October 3, Hitler boasted that his troops had conquered an area of Russian territory twice the size of the 1933 Germany. A few days later, another 600,000 Russian soldiers were captured, and Germany began to claim that the war in Russia was over. Nazi soldiers were just 80 miles from Moscow now.

Again, Hitler and his generals could not agree on a strategy. His armies were fanned out over a front a thousand miles long, deep within Russia, and no clear idea of which part of Russia to proceed into had emerged. The result was confusion; winter came and, in spite of their military successes, the Germans had taken neither Moscow nor Leningrad, and found themselves deep within Russia.

Bitter cold assailed Hitler's troops, who had no winter

clothing to protect them. Grimly the Nazis battled on toward Moscow, but a final attempt on December 2 to reach the capital was repulsed as snow drifted down. Then, on December 6, the Russians unexpectedly opened a counteroffensive. All summer and fall they had been retreating. Now 100 fresh divisions appeared and began to hurl the invaders back from Moscow. Hitler's dream of conquering Russia by the end of 1941 was doomed to disappointment. The question now was whether he would conquer Russia at all.

The day after the Russian counterattack began, Japan attacked Pearl Harbor and the United States entered the war. So sneak attacks by Germany and Japan in 1941 had brought both Russia and the U. S. into the war. Time would show that these were both major miscalculations on the part of the Axis.

Hitler's troops in Russia were on the edge of panic that December. They recalled Napoleon's retreat from Moscow under similar circumstances in 1812—a long, harrowing, deadly march through frozen Russia. They were afraid the same fate awaited them. But Hitler performed one of his miracles of exhortation. "Stand firm," he ordered. "There will be no retreat. In the spring we will conquer Russia."

The Germans settled down in Russia to wait out the winter. Those Nazi generals who recommended retreat were removed from command and court-martialed. The long winter months passed, thousands of German soldiers dying of the cold. Neither the Russian counteroffensive nor the effects of frostbite broke the German line, and by spring Hitler was ready to resume his offensive. The campaign so far had been costly, but victory was still within his grasp. In a speech on April 26, 1942, Hitler boasted that he had succeeded where Napoleon had failed: "A world struggle was decided during the winter. . . . We have mastered a destiny which broke another man a hundred and thirty years ago."

Hitler's empire had now reached its greatest point. From

the Arctic Sea to the Nile, from Brittany to deep in Russia, he held sway. Only England resisted him in Europe. On the other side of the world his Japanese allies had made themselves masters of the Pacific and of much of Asia. But the turning point was coming.

Hitler's spring offensive against Russia in 1942 was two-pronged. One wing of his army marched eastward toward the Volga River and the city of Stalingrad, while the other wing cut toward the south, and the rich oilfields of the Caucasus. Here, Hitler's impatience and greed undid him. By splitting his army, he failed to gain either Stalingrad or the oilfields. A single assault at one place or the other would have yielded almost certain victory.

Hitler would not listen to advice, though. His generals pointed out the danger of his exposed position. A report told him that the Russians could throw an army of a million and a quarter men at him at Stalingrad, and half a million in the Caucasus, and that the Russians were building 1,200 tanks a month. "Hitler flew at the man who was reading, with clenched fists and foam in the corners of his mouth," an eyewitness wrote, and forbade him to read such idiotic twaddle."

By September 1942, the double German advance had been halted in both places. When the commander of his Stalingrad force recommended breaking off the attack, Hitler removed him from command and replaced him. When the offensive in the Caucasus bogged down, Hitler sent one of his key officers, General Jodl, to investigate. Jodl returned with word that the offensive was hopeless. Hitler replaced him.

Firing generals could not conceal the ultimate truth: Hitler had reached the peak of his power. From here to the end of the war he would be forced to take the defensive. Until now, he had been calling the tune, but no more.

All through the summer of 1942 the Germans had been

advancing at a terrific rate toward the Caucasus. But in August they started to run low on fuel, and to enter mountainous country where progress was slow. Meanwhile the troops making the push toward Stalingrad were being stopped. They were hampered by the stubborn Russian resistance, and by the fact that so many badly needed men were off in the Caucasus. Still, the Germans inched forward, pounding the defenders brutally and forcing them slowly back toward the city of Stalingrad.

This was no war of spears and javelins, nor of swords, nor of one-shot rifles and bayonets. It was a war of tanks and heavy guns. But the basic idea of battle had not changed over thousands of years, only the weapons. To encircle the enemy, to drive him into confusion, to break his ranks and make him flee—those were the objectives, as always.

As the Russians fell back on Stalingrad, their own position, as defenders, became stronger. They were packed tightly together, now, and the Germans had little room to maneuver. Whereas earlier the Russian forces had been strung out over hundreds of miles, now they had come together in one point: the city of Stalingrad.

The critical day was October 14, 1942. The Russians had their backs virtually at the Volga now. It seemed as though one powerful German thrust would scatter the defenders and send the key city to defeat.

The Russians held, however. And now the tide gradually began to turn. The weather was growing cold, and the Germans, remembering the horror of the winter of 1941–2, dreaded a second bout with a Russian December. Their numbers had been thinned during the long campaign. The German forces, divided and hard pressed at both places, had little flexibility. And they were growing weary.

The Russians were preparing their counterstroke. They launched it on November 19. Three Russian Army groups, commanded by Generals Eremenko, Rokossovsky and Vatu-tin, struck back along a broad front to the north and south of Stalingrad. Rokossovsky, with three armored corps, four cav-alry corps, and 21 infantry divisions, led the counterattack. The next day Eremenko, with two armored corps and nine infantry divisions, swung out and through the Germans and linked with him. The German Sixth Army, 200,000 strong, found itself encircled. Vatutin's forces tightened the pincers.

The German general, Paulus, sent word of his predicament to Hitler, who gave the same advice he had offered the winter before: "Stand firm. Fight to the last man."

Paulus pointed out that he was surrounded. Hitler told him bluntly to fight his way out of the trap. He sent one of his ablest generals, Field Marshal von Manstein, to Paulus' aid. Manstein's assignment was to break the Russian pincers—not to allow Paulus to retreat, but to permit him to resume the attack on Stalingrad.

Manstein opened his offensive on December 12. His plan, devised by Hitler, was to strike at Eremenko's army first, then to smash Rokossovsky's forces while Paulus attacked Stalin-grad. By December 21, Manstein was within 30 miles of Paulus' trapped army.

Then the advance ran out of steam. Vatutin, the third Russian commander, hit Manstein with unexpected strength. Both Paulus' troops and Manstein's were low on supplies, low on ammunition, low on morale. Hitler ordered Paulus to stand his ground and let Manstein free him, but Manstein was un-able to do so. Again and again Paulus sent word to Hitler that the situation was hopeless, only to be told to hold the line until spring without retreating.

Hitler's other offensive, in the Caucasus, was going equally poorly. By January 1943, Hitler finally came to see that if he attempted to maintain both armies, he would suffer a double defeat. And so, reluctantly, he gave the order for the army in the Caucasus to retreat. It was the first time in the war thus far that the Germans had had to fall back from a position.

Manstein was sent to cover the Caucasus retreat. This maneuver saved hundreds of thousands of Nazi soldiers from capture, but left the Stalingrad army in a worse position than ever before. The temperature dropped to 28 below zero. Typhus and dysentery took thousands of lives in the German camp. Medical supplies were all but exhausted. Rations were cut again and again.

On January 8, Rokossovsky called on the Germans to surrender. Paulus, bound by Hitler's orders, had to refuse, whereupon the Russians launched a general assault on the trapped army. Finally Paulus sent a despairing message to Hitler, telling the Fuehrer that his troops could no longer bear their sufferings.

Hitler's reply was blunt: "Capitulation is impossible. The Sixth Army will do its historic duty at Stalingrad until the last man, in order to make possible the reconstruction of the Eastern Front."

On January 25, the Russians captured the only remaining German airfield in the area. This cut off any possibility that fresh provisions could reach the Sixth Army, and now surrender could not be long away. On January 31, Hitler promoted Paulus to the rank of field marshal, hoping to buy his loyalty with the bribe.

But promotions could not save the Sixth Army. That same day, Paulus sent word that the Russians were upon them, and that he was surrendering. He had held out for months under the most harrowing of conditions and, in fact, his staunch stand had saved the German retreat from the Caucasus, since if he had surrendered earlier the Russians would have been free to fall upon the retreating Nazis in the south. Now Paulus could hold out no longer. With 23 of his generals, 2,000 junior officers, 90,000 soldiers, and 40,000 noncombatants, he yielded to Rokossovsky. The Stalingrad campaign had cost Germany more than 100,000 men, and tremendous quantities of arms and ammunition.

Hitler raged at the news of Paulus' surrender. "The man should have shot himself, just as the old commanders who threw themselves on their swords when they saw their cause was lost," he blustered. The Fuehrer could not understand how Paulus could have dared to surrender after being promoted. "What hurts me most, personally, is that I promoted him to field marshal. I wanted to give him this final satisfaction. That's the last field marshal I shall appoint in this war. . . . So many people have to die, and then a man like that besmirches the heroism of so many others at the last minute."

Hitler's words were the ravings of a madman. But, then, the whole Russian campaign had been lunacy. With the example of Napoleon before him, Hitler had ventured into Russia and, like Napoleon, had been hurled back with heavy losses. For both dictators, the Russian campaign marked the beginning of the end.

Stalingrad was a decisive battle in two ways. First, it shattered the morale of the German Army, so that for the remaining two and a half years of the European war the Germans were constantly on the defensive, constantly drawing back. From 1939 to 1942 the Nazis had gloried in the intoxicating awareness of their own invincibility. Stalingrad robbed them of that feeling. Hitler's men were never the same. His generals saw all too plainly that the Fuehrer was insane, that his strategy was worthless, after the Stalingrad fiasco.

Secondly, Stalingrad transferred that myth of invincibility from the Germans to the Russians. The Russians had performed with tremendous heroism; they had stood firm, they had broken a heretofore unstoppable German army. From that time on they fought with a sense of destiny, of overpowering self-confidence.

The spirit of Stalingrad has never really left the Russians. That great victory has buoyed their spirits for more than two decades. Much of Russia's confident, cockily aggressive attitude of the post-war era stems directly from the lesson they learned at Stalingrad, the lesson of their own military might. (Strangely, in view of the symbolic meaning of Stalingrad to the Russians, they changed the city's name in 1961 during the downgrading of Stalin. It is now called Volgagrad.)

Time and again we have seen how a single morale-shattering defeat can end the dominance of a major power. The Persians were never quite the same after Marathon, the Arabs after Tours, the Turks after Lepanto. Stalingrad meant the end of Hitler's hope of world empire.

Why, then, did he attack Russia in the first place, in 1941? Why venture into a needless war?

First, Hitler believed that the Russians were much weaker than they turned out to be. He committed the fatal error of underestimating his enemy.

Second, Hitler overestimated his own forces. He was sure that his troops could smash Russia in a single season. And so he sent armies into Russia without even bothering to work out a coherent strategy.

Third, Hitler was a man of irrational actions. His rise to power was based on hysterical, almost insane maneuvers that happened to succeed. The Russian campaign simply happened not to succeed. He made his back-stabbing attack on Russia because, drunk with earlier triumphs, he could not imagine being defeated.

A wiser man would have waited, and finished off Great Britain before opening a new front in the east. Britain might well have fallen to the Nazis by October or November, 1941. Then Hitler could have sprung his attack on Russia the following April, and completed his conquest of Europe.

But a wiser man would not have engaged on a career like Hitler's in the first place. Hitler's madness led him to start the war, and it was the same madness that caused him to launch his suicidal attack on Russia, resulting in the climactic and decisive German defeat at Stalingrad that signaled the downfall of Nazi Germany.

Aᴺᴰ so we come to the end of our account of the 15 decisive battles of the world. We cannot carry the story beyond Stalingrad, because that was the last *decisive* battle the world has seen. Since 1945, the United States and the Soviet Union have been locked in a new kind of war, a Cold War, a war of nerves rather than of bullets. The only old-fashioned war on a large scale to be fought in the Cold War era, that of Korea, ended in stalemate.

Perhaps there will never again be a battle that can be called decisive. Let us hope so, for new weapons have made war something quite different from the war understood by William the Conqueror or Charles Martel. The next battle, if it ever comes, may be decisive indeed—deciding the fate of all mankind forever.

It remains for some future historian, if there are any, to choose the decisive moments of the conflict of the post 1945 world. We do not have enough perspective on our own times to make any such choices. Fifty, a hundred years must go by, and then we can look back and accurately name the turning points in this strange undeclared war without bloodshed.

In 1851, as he completed his *Fifteen Decisive Battles of the World,* Sir Edward Creasy was able to remark that there was no longer war in the world. He wrote, "We have not (and long may we be without) the stern excitement of martial strife, and we see no captive standards of our European neighbors brought in triumph to our shrines. But we behold an infinitely prouder spectacle. We see the banners of every civilized nation waving over the arena of our competition with each other, in the arts that minister to our race's support and happiness, and not to its suffering and destruction."

This book can come to no such glowing conclusion. We live today in a precarious age where maddened men can choose to destroy us all. Under such circumstances the clashing of swords at Hastings sounds tinny indeed, the sound of guns at Waterloo becomes a distant and meaningless pop of toy weapons. But the battles of the past show an encouraging pattern. For all the fears and tensions of today, we have progressed. Men are healthier than ever before, men have greater comfort than ever before, and—even in those parts of the world behind the Iron Curtain—men are freer than ever before. We have harnessed the forces of nature and built a glittering society of incredible complexity and brilliance. Starvation, poverty, ignorance are retreating everywhere from year to year. And now we have begun to reach outward toward the stars.

The picture, then, is not entirely bleak. Progress has been made in the 2,500 years since Marathon. Now that such monstrous powers of self-destruction are in our grasp, humanity faces its greatest test. We must look forward to the future with uncertainty—but also with hope.

BIBLIOGRAPHY

Compiling a bibliography for a book of this sort is a little bit like trying to put together a bibliography of all human history. It's an impossible task—and even if it could be done, it would not be of much use to the interested reader who simply wants to go on to a more detailed account of the battles described in here.

What I have done, instead, is to list one or two books dealing with each of the 15 battles. In all cases these are books that I myself consulted. However, I also made use of certain magazine articles and other brief material which could not easily be obtained by someone looking for further information, and which therefore are not listed here.

Two general books on military history belong in the library of anyone interested in this subject. They are:

A Military History of the Western World, by Major J. F. C. Fuller (3 volumes, 1954)

Fifteen Decisive Battles of the World, by E. S. Creasy (First published 1851—still in print in various editions)

As for the individual battles, these are the books I would recommend for further study:

MARATHON

The classic ancient account is that of Herodotus. It is available in English in many translations.

A very good, though rare, book on the Greek and Persian struggle is G. B. Grundy's *The Great Persian War* (1901). There is also a good description of the battle in the *Cambridge Ancient History,* volume 4 (1926).

ZAMA

The ancient accounts are found in the works of Livy and Polybius, both available in English translations.

A good book on Carthage is *Daily Life in the Time of Hannibal,* by Picard (1958).

ACTIUM

The ancient account is by Dio Cassius. For modern versions of the battle, see the *Cambridge Ancient History* and the first volume of General Fuller's book.

ADRIANOPLE

The story of the fall of Rome is nowhere better told than in Gibbon's *Decline and Fall of the Roman Empire*. General Fuller also devotes considerable space to this battle.

TOURS

See the *Cambridge Medieval History,* volume 2 (1936). A modern biography of Charles Martel is badly needed. For background on the Arab conquests of the period, see Carl Brockelmann's *History of the Islamic Peoples* (1947).

HASTINGS

Few battles in English history have attracted so much wordage. One good book out of multitudes is Sir James H. Ramsay's *The Foundations of England* (Oxford University Press). See also Creasy, Fuller, and any good history of England—such as that by Trevelyan, or Winston Churchill's *History of the English-Speaking Peoples*.

ORLÉANS

See General Fuller and the *Cambridge Medieval History*. Bernard Shaw's *Saint Joan*, though it is fictional and takes certain liberties with history, gives a vivid picture of the period.

LEPANTO

The standard book is *Don John of Austria*, by Sir W. Stirling Maxwell (1883), but this will not be easy to find. General Fuller tells the story in great detail, however.

THE ARMADA

The most recent of many books on this subject should be definitive for quite a while to come. It is *The Armada*, by Garrett Mattingly (1959).

BLENHEIM

There are two great books on this battle and on the Duke of Marlborough's career: *The Wars of Marlborough,* by Frank Taylor (2 volumes, 1921) and Sir Winston Churchill's account of his own celebrated ancestor, *Marlborough, His Life and Times* (4 volumes, 1933–38).

THE PLAINS OF ABRAHAM

The best accounts of this battle are in two scarce books on the history of Quebec: *Old Quebec,* by Parker and Bryan (1903) and *The Province of Quebec*, by J. C. Sutherland (1922). But there are good versions in the *Encyclopedia Britannica*, in Fuller, and in Fletcher Pratt's *Decisive Battles of the World* (1951).

VALCOUR ISLAND

The source here is Christopher Ward's two-volume *The War of the Revolution* (1952). An entire chapter is devoted to this otherwise obscure battle.

WATERLOO

One volume out of hundreds on Waterloo is E. F. Becke's *Napoleon and Waterloo* (1914). Creasy and Fuller are both particularly good on Waterloo. And be sure to read Stendhal's matchless fictional description of the battle in the opening chapters of *The Charterhouse of Parma*.

GETTYSBURG

Who could select a single volume on the Civil War? I put forth Bruce Catton's *This Hallowed Ground* (1956) in the awareness that many others could be recommended just as strongly. A more extensive account of the battle is to be found in Douglas Freeman's massive *R. E. Lee, a Biography* (4 volumes, 1935).

STALINGRAD

See Sir Winston Churchill's *The Hinge of Fate* (1950) and Alan Bullock's *Hitler: A Study in Tyranny* (revised edition, 1959). Fuller is also excellent on this battle.

Index

Abd-ar-Rahman, 61, 62, 63, 64-65
Actium, battle of, 43-46
Adams, John, 143
Adrianople, battle of, 54-57
Aeneas, 24-25
Aeschylus, 20
Agrippa, 42, 43, 44, 46
Alan, Count, 77
Alaric, 58
Alatheus, 54, 55
Alavivus, 52
Alexander the Great, 24
Alfred, King of England, 67, 68
Ali Pasha, 102, 103, 104, 105
Allen, Ethan, 142
American Revolution, 141, 142, 153
Amherst, Lord Jeffrey, 129, 134, 135, 139
Angles, 67, 68
Anne, Queen of England, 119
Antietam, battle of, 169
Antony, Mark, 39-46, 47
Arabia and the Arabs, 59-60, 61-65, 96, 97-98
Arbela, battle of, 24
Aristides, 20, 21
Arnold, Benedict, 142-43, 144-53
Arruntius, 44
Artaphernes, 17, 18
Assyria and the Assyrians, 13-14
Athens and the Athenians, 16-24
Augustulus, Romulus, 49

Barbarigo, Admiral, 103
Barclay de Tolly, 158
Baudricourt, Robert de, 87
Bedford, Duke of, 84, 86, 90
Benedict XV, Pope, 95
Blenheim, battle of, 122-27
Blücher, Marshal, 158-66
Bonaparte, Napoleon, 154-66
Braddock, General George, 129
Bradstreet, Colonel, 130
Bull Run, battle of, 169

Caesar, Gaius Julius, 39-40
Callimachus, 18, 19, 21
Cambyses II, 14
Canidius, 42, 46
Cannae, battle of, 29, 32

Canute, King of England, 68
Carleton, Sir Guy, 144, 145, 147-52
Carthage and the Carthaginians, 25-26, 27-37
Celts, 67, 68
Cervantes, Miguel, 105
Chancellorsville, battle of, 169, 170
Charlemagne, 66, 68
Charleroi, battle of, 159
Charles V, Emperor, 97
Charles VI, King of France, 84, 94
Charles VII, King of France, 84, 85, 86, 87-88, 92-93, 94
Charles Martel, 60-66, 96
Chattanooga, battle of, 169
Christian League, 98-99, 101, 105
Churchill, Winston S., 127, 177-78
Civil War, American, 167-75
Cleopatra, Queen of Egypt, 40, 41, 42, 43, 45, 46
Clotaire, IV, 61
Cold War, 187
Colonna, Marco Antonio, 99, 101, 102
Confederate States of America, 168
Contarini, Marco, 103
Continental Congress, 143, 144
Cordova, Philip de, 113
Crassus, 39
Creasy, Sir Edward S., 11, 70, 115, 126, 141, 188
Cutts, Lord, 124, 125
Cyprus, 98, 99, 101, 105
Cyrus the Great, 14

Danes, 68
Darius I, 14, 15, 16-17, 22
Datis, 17, 21, 22
Davis, Jefferson, 168
D'Erlon, General, 161, 162, 164
Dido, Queen, 25
Dinwiddie, Governor, 129
Dio Cassius, 28, 44, 45, 46
Doria, Admiral, 103, 104
Drake, Sir Francis, 107, 108, 109-10, 111, 112, 114
Durell, Admiral, 130, 131

Eastern Roman Empire, 51, 58, 59, 60, 96

Edward III, King of England, 83-84
Edward the Confessor, 68, 70, 71
Egbert, King of Wessex, 67
Egypt, 39-40, 41, 42, 46, 47, 155
Elba, 156
Elizabeth, Queen of England, 107, 108-09, 110-11, 114
England and the English, 67-82, 83-95, 107-17, 118-27, 128-40, 142-52, 155, 160-66, 176, 177, 180, 185-86
English Channel, 109, 111, 114
Eremenko, General, 182
Eretria, 17, 18
Ethelred the Unready, 68
Eudo, Duke of Aquitania, 61-62, 65
Eugene, Prince of Austria, 122, 124, 125, 126
Eunapius, 51
Eustace of Boulogne, 77
Ewell, General Richard S., 170, 171, 172, 173

Fabius, 29
Ferdinand, King of Spain, 97
Fortesque, J. W., 138
France and the French, 68, 83-95, 118-26, 128-40, 154-66, 176
Franks, 60-66
Fredericksburg, battle of, 169
Fritigern, 52, 54, 55-56, 58
Frobisher, Sir Martin, 107, 109
Fuller, Major General J. F. C., 11, 23, 82, 100, 103, 105, 117, 120, 127, 141

Gallisonière, Governor de la, 128-29
Gates, General Horatio, 144, 145, 147
Gaul and the Gauls, 26, 28, 32, 34, 38, 39, 50, 61-66
George II, King of England, 130
Germany and the Germans, 176-86
Gettysburg, battle of, 169, 171-75
Gibbs-Smith, Charles H., 80

192

THE AUTHOR

ROBERT SILVERBERG has been a full-time free lance writer since he graduated from Columbia University in 1956. However, he began writing professionally in 1953 and in 1955 he had his first book published. Originally specializing in science fiction, Mr. Silverberg currently writes mostly non-fiction paperback originals as well as books for young people. His hobbies include travel and collecting classical records. He, his wife and their three cats live in a huge, book-filled old house once owned by Fiorello LaGuardia, in Riverdale, New York.